EP Sport Series

* All About Judo
* Badminton
* Basketball
  Conditioning for Sport
  Field Athletics
* Football
* Golf
  Hockey for Men and Women
  Improve your Riding
  Learning to Swim
  Modern Riding
* Netball
* Orienteering
  Rock Climbing
  Sailing
  Snooker
* Squash Rackets
  Start Motor Cruising
* Table Tennis
* Tennis up to Tournament
    Standard
* Track Athletics
  Underwater Swimming
  Volleyball
  Wildwater Canoeing
  Women's Gymnastics

At the time of publication of
this edition the asterisked titles
are available in paperback as
well as hardback

ep sport

cricket

Keith Andrew

Bob Carter

Les Lenham

Regional National Coaches for
the National Cricket Association

Acknowledgements

The authors would like to acknowledge with thanks the assistance of the following in the preparation of this book:

G. O. Allen, M.B.E., for his invaluable technical assistance.

Brian Everette, for the filming of the sequence photographs.

The following for supplying the action shots and allowing them to be reproduced:

Birmingham Post and Mail (p. 76).
Central Press Photos Ltd (pp. 65, 110).
Ken Kelly (pp. 10, 13, 21, 24, 33, 38, 44, 50, 52, 56, 63, 78, 91, 96, 99, 101).
S & G Press Agency Ltd (Frontispiece, p. 8).

The Authors

The authors of this book, Keith Andrew, Bob Carter and Les Lenham, are all national coaches employed by the National Cricket Association. Their combined experience covers school, club, league, Services, County, Limited-Over and international cricket. By lucky coincidence or design, one is a batsman, one a bowler and the third a wicketkeeper. They have coaching experience ranging over four continents at levels from school, youth international and county championship.

The object of the book is to present the techniques of the game in as simple a form as possible for the teacher or beginner and also to enable the more experienced player to check his technique for faults and then eradicate them. It is also hoped that the chapter on captaincy will stimulate thought as well as giving guidance to all present and potential captains.

ISBN 0 7158 0574 6 (cased edition)
ISBN 0 7158 0642 4 (limp edition)

Published by EP Publishing Ltd, East Ardsley, Wakefield, West Yorkshire. 1978

Reprinted 1981

Text set in 11/12 pt Monophoto Univers, printed by photolithography and bound in Great Britain by G. Beard & Son Ltd, Brighton

Contents

Preface

Cricket has long been regarded as a game in which a consistently high standard of performance is very difficult to achieve. For the gifted few its skills come naturally, but for the great majority success can only be realised through hard practice and experience, allied to the benefits of good coaching.

Countless books have been written about cricket, many of which describe the techniques of great individual players. Only as recently as 1952 with the publication of the *M.C.C. Coaching Book* was there an endeavour to analyse in great detail the game's basic skills. The subsequent formation of the M.C.C. Youth Cricket Association in the same year helped to unite coaching expertise throughout the country. Since then, interest in coaching, and through this the increased desire to improve techniques, has blossomed. In the intervening years thousands of young cricket enthusiasts have qualified as coaches through study and practice and have taught the game generally along similar lines in schools and in clubs. It was obvious, even before 1952, going back to the beginning of the game, that the best results, particularly in batting, tended to come from environments where playing conditions were good and backed by knowledgeable and experienced instruction.

The formation of the National Cricket Association in 1967, with a brief to represent the best interests of all cricket outside the first-class game, brought another great step forward in communication, as it continued the work so well started by M.C.C. For the first time all forms of club and school cricket were fully represented on the Cricket Council, the game's governing body. Now, with the backing of the Government through the Sports Council, M.C.C., the Test and County Cricket Board and, not least, its member clubs, the N.C.A. is in a position of strength from which considerable progress in the development of the game should be possible.

Significantly, many areas of the game are already showing great benefits although, and rightly so, N.C.A have given priority to the development of their National Coaching Scheme. Administered through the N.C.A. County Associations in co-operation with the N.C.A. National Coaches, who cover all regions of the country, a nationwide network of qualified coaches is progressively increasing in effectiveness. The ideal of a qualified coach being available to every school and every club is still an ideal, but the day is not far off when any youngster who wishes to play cricket will be able to do so with the benefit of enthusiastic and knowledgeable guidance.

Many uninformed people tend to scoff at the word 'coaching' thinking of it solely as a method of producing efficient conformity of attitude and physical movement, with accent placed on doing everything in one way only. This is far from the truth.

Coaching embraces all the facets of cricket development, particularly amongst youngsters, and takes in much wider aspects of the game. A good coach must have a sense of humour, enthusiasm, the ability to encourage, together with a knowledge of teaching techniques. The good coach will appreciate that cricket is more than a game between two teams of eleven players, he will know the history of the game and be able to communicate the magic of its folk lore. He will be well versed in the very latest developments in the game, from the rules of six-a-side cricket to the use of non-turf pitches in clubs and schools. He will realise that coaching cannot be and should not be conducted in the nets only; and that if he has a duty, it will be to ensure that in a coaching session everyone will be involved all the time and that all his charges get a 'fair crack of the whip', regardless of their ability.

With these thoughts on coaching very much in mind, N.C.A. welcome the co-operation of EP Publishing Limited in the production of this book. Other publications adequately cover many of the aspects of coaching previously mentioned. For the first time, techniques of the game, demonstrated by N.C.A. National Coaches, are presented in sequences so that the various skills can be clearly studied and analysed. The use of a 35 mm high-speed cine camera with an exposure of forty-eight frames per second has made this possible. Each photograph within a sequence achieves a clarity that entitles the book to be recognised not only as a complement to other N.C.A. publications, but as a visual aid within itself.

The Game

A game in progress . . . the total attention of all the fielders is on the batsman as he plays the ball

The Playing Area

Cricket in England is usually played on turf which has been cut short so that the ball can travel over the surface of the ground without being slowed unduly by long grass. There are no fixed limits as to the total area involved but a visible or physical barrier—white line, rope, fence, etc.—which is called 'the boundary', indicates where the playing area finishes. Most clubs try to arrange their fixtures so that for important matches the boundary is between 50 and 90 yd (45 and 82 m) from the centre of the pitch.

The Pitch

The pitch, often referred to incorrectly as the wicket, is an area 22 yd (20.12 m) long and 10 ft (3.05 m) wide. The English player expects this to consist of a level, smooth, hard, compact surface from which nearly all the blades of grass have been removed by very close mowing.

Overseas fewer pitches are of turf; a large number are constructed of concrete or water-bound porous materials with a mat of natural or man-made fibre on top. These

PITCH MARKINGS AND DIMENSIONS

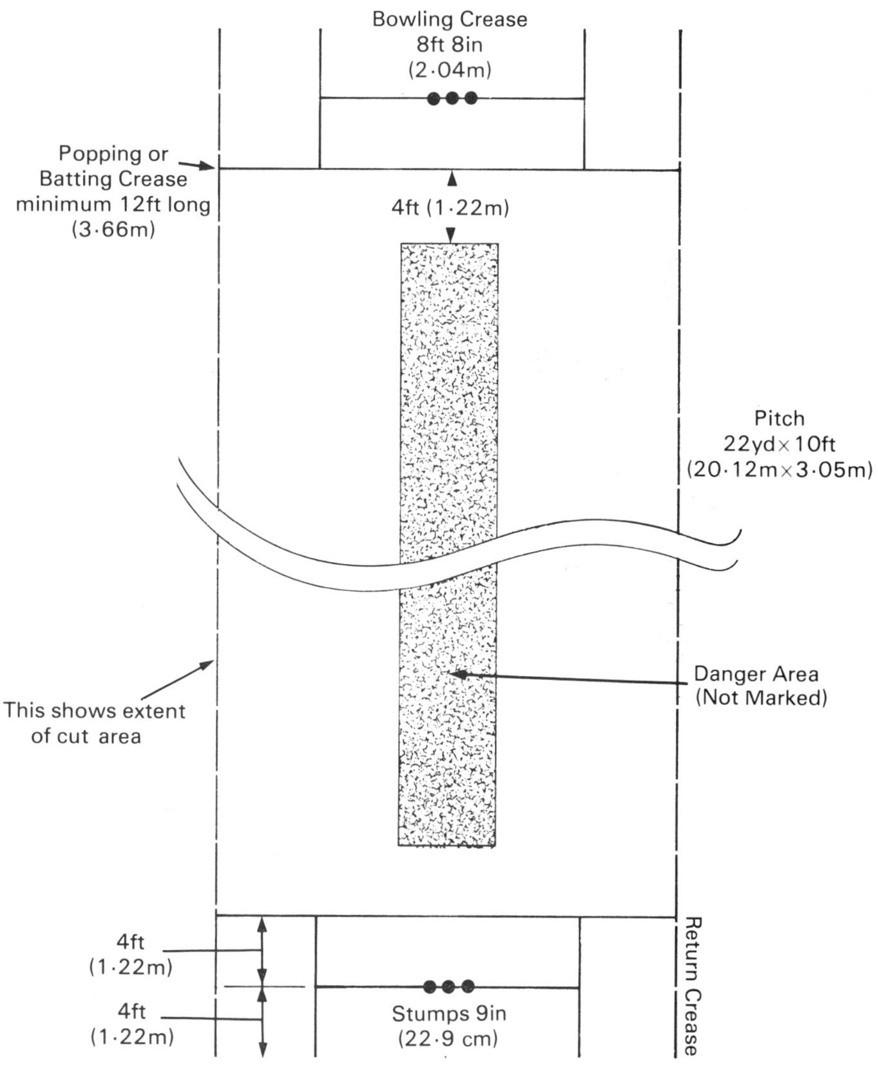

Bowling Crease
8ft 8in
(2·04m)

Popping or Batting Crease minimum 12ft long (3·66m)

4ft (1·22m)

Pitch 22yd × 10ft (20·12m × 3·05m)

This shows extent of cut area

Danger Area (Not Marked)

Return Crease

4ft (1·22m)

4ft (1·22m)

Stumps 9in (22·9 cm)

All measurements taken from back edge or inside of Crease

playing surfaces may not have all the characteristics of a true turf pitch but are preferable to poor turf as the ball bounces consistently. As a result players can confidently judge the movement of the ball and make allowances for it when playing a stroke.

To prepare a good turf pitch, time, knowledge and good weather are essential. Because of the expense involved and the uncertainty of British weather many schools and some clubs now play on non-turf pitches, whilst others are seriously considering laying down such pitches.

The Wicket

There are two wickets in cricket, one at either end of the pitch, each consisting of three stumps and two bails. The stumps are driven into the ground on the back edge of the bowling crease, so that the ball will not pass between any two stumps without disturbing them. The overall width of the wicket is 9 in. (228 mm) and when the two bails are placed in the grooves on top of the stumps the vertical height is 2 ft 4½ in. (724 mm).

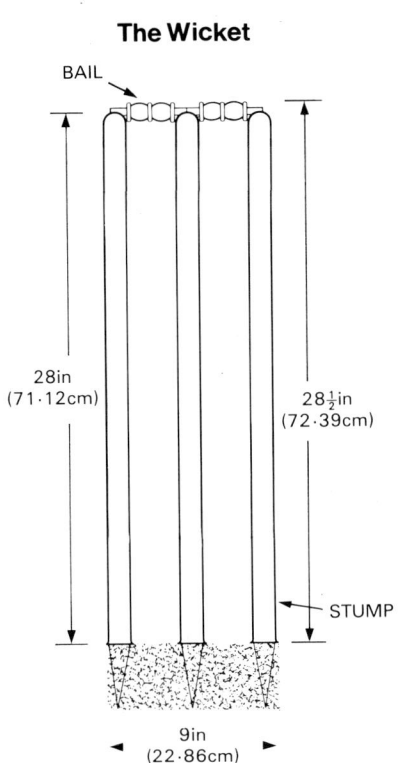

The Wicket

BAIL

28in (71·12cm)

28½in (72·39cm)

STUMP

9in (22·86cm)

Umpires

There are two umpires whose job is to officiate and above all to see fair play. One, the bowling umpire, stands in line with the wickets and behind that from which the bowler will deliver the ball. The other, the square-leg umpire, stands level with the batting crease at the other end of the pitch and some distance from it.

Position of the 'bowling' umpire

Equipment
BATS

Probably the most expensive and coveted piece of a player's equipment is his bat. This should be personally selected for size and balance as many faults in batting technique can

Bats

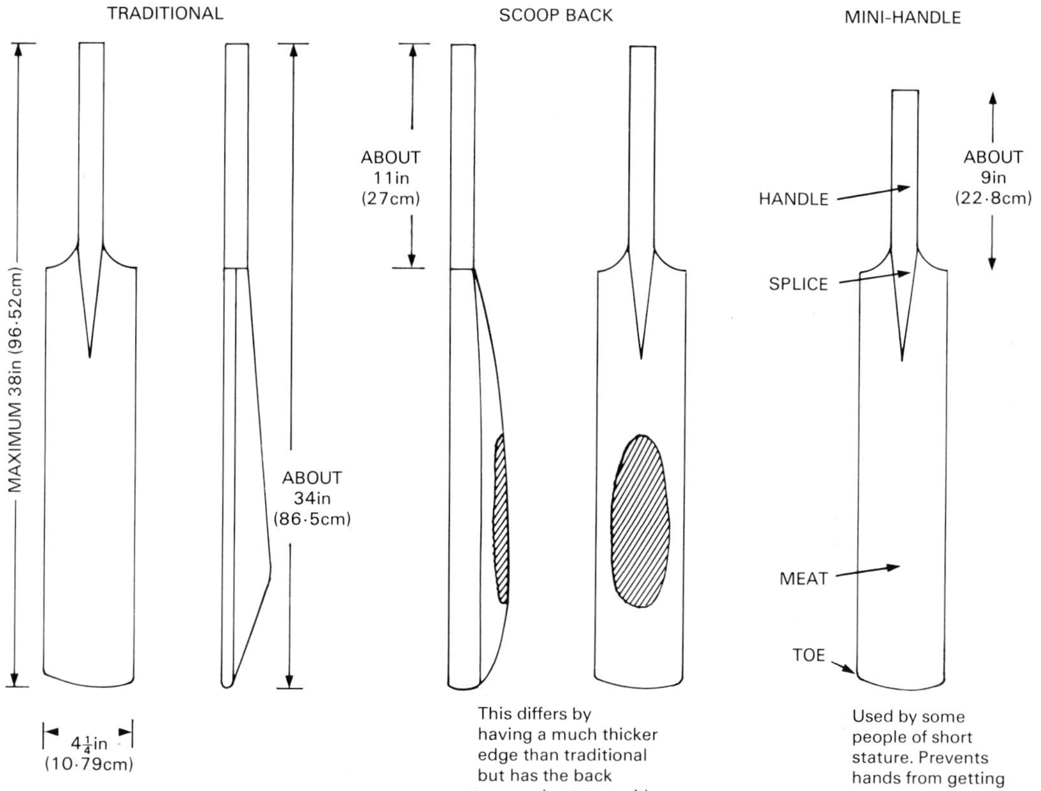

TRADITIONAL

MAXIMUM 38in (96·52cm)

ABOUT 34in (86·5cm)

4¼in (10·79cm)

SCOOP BACK

ABOUT 11in (27cm)

This differs by having a much thicker edge than traditional but has the back scooped out to avoid excessive weight.

MINI-HANDLE

ABOUT 9in (22·8cm)

HANDLE

SPLICE

MEAT

TOE

Used by some people of short stature. Prevents hands from getting too far apart.

be traced back to using one which is either too large or too heavy. If a player cannot pick up the bat comfortably with only the top hand and that in the correct position, it is too heavy.

The handle should have a little give in it and a grip firmly glued on to it. The only real test of a bat is to use it, but a guide to how it will react can be ascertained by knocking up

a ball on it; the ball springs off good bats, poor bats feel 'wooden' and dull.

Owners should take note of the manufacturers' instructions regarding care, as many modern bats do not require oil. Those that do only need a wipe over with a rag lightly impregnated with linseed oil, but keep the oil off the splice.

Damaged bats should be professionally repaired as

quickly as possible since further use may result in total breakage.

PROTECTIVE EQUIPMENT

Whether you are a batsman or a wicketkeeper, it is essential that that you wear good quality, light-weight and well-fitting pads so that rapid movement is not hampered. However, you must not sacrifice protection, particularly of your knees and

Various types of batting gloves

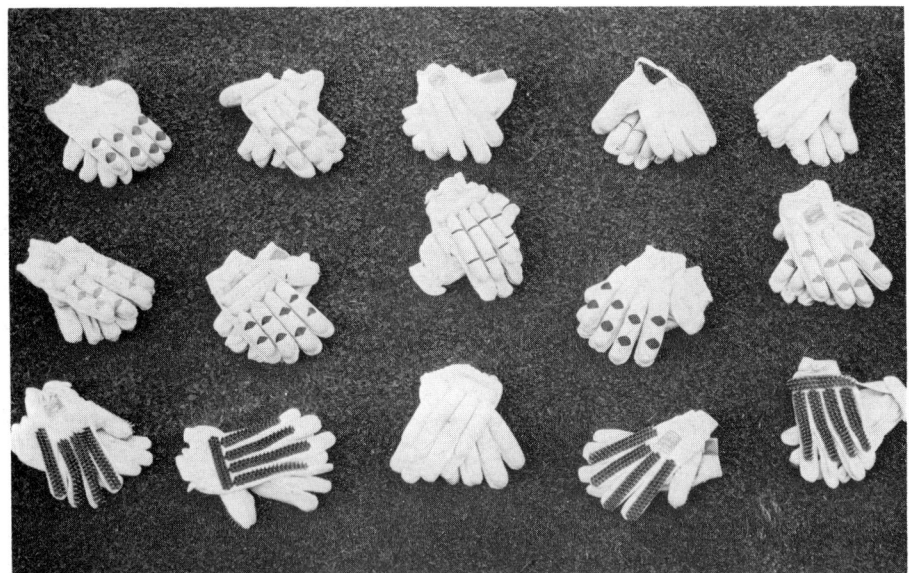

Wicketkeeping gloves, inners, thigh pad and various protectors

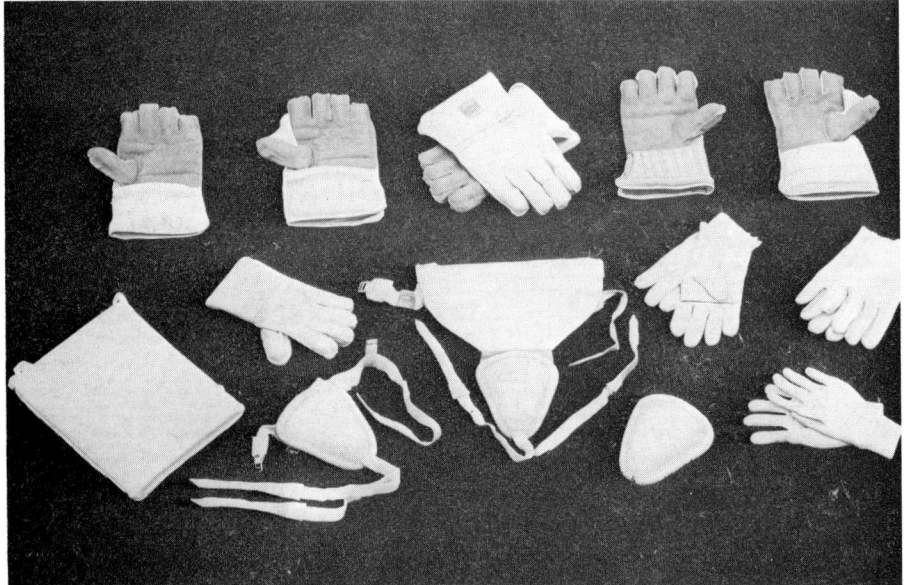

shins, in deciding whether pads are too heavy or bulky.

Once buckled, the strap can be cut so that there is no superfluous amount flapping and making the batsman look untidy.

When a batsman faces fast bowlers or on pitches when he expects the ball to bounce higher than usual, a thigh pad worn inside the trousers of the front leg is a great aid to confidence. These can be fibre-glass moulded to fit the leg with padding underneath or firm rubber inside a piece of material. both types need to be tied securely, without metal buckles which could injure the batsman if struck by the ball. All wicketkeepers and batsmen must wear a 'box' or protector. Though plastic ones are favoured by some players others still put their trust in metal shields padded round the edge.

Batting gloves are of many types—open palm, wrap-around gloves or mitts—so that everyone should be able to feel comfortable. The essential thing is that the protection offered covers the knuckles, thumb of the bottom hand and back of the hands.

The end of a hook stroke. Note the batsman's equipment—pads neatly buckled, no flapping straps, thigh pad nessary for fast or bouncy pitches, well-fitting gloves and a cap to assist sighting the ball in all weather conditions ▶

Clothing

Footwear is the most vital part of any player's equipment: if the feet are not comfortable and the grip on the ground not secure, then fast reaction and concentration are adversely affected. Many players now elect to play in light, properly studded shoes, although a light boot is still preferred by most bowlers, as it gives support to the ankles. In either case they should be large enough to allow the user to wear at least one pair of thick woollen socks. For extra comfort some bowlers wear two pairs and, as additional cushioning when bowling on very hard pitches, insert rubber heel cushions in their boots.

Regular checks, preferably well before each game, should be made of all equipment but especially of the spikes and laces in the boots. Worn items should be replaced and the footwear cleaned prior to playing. After a game mud should be scraped off and it is useful to have a pair of boot bags which will prevent other equipment from getting mud or rust stains.

Trousers should be purchased bearing in mind that they are for

an activity which requires the wearer to bend, stretch, run, etc. This may mean that fashion has to be dispensed with up to a point.

Bowlers' and wicketkeepers' shirts need plenty of width across the shoulders, so you may well have to buy a size larger than you would normally wear. The best shirts are those which are thick enough to absorb perspiration. But even these may not prevent a perspiring bowler getting a chill when a cold wind is blowing the shirt against his muscles. A vest helps to prevent this as also do good-quality sweaters, which should be donned on any occasion when a chill might occur. Remember that a cold muscle is one which is likely to be damaged if brought into action rapidly.

Finally each player should provide himself with a cap. Though many prefer not to wear one, there are times when the sun can be very troublesome and wearing a cap on these occasions makes looking towards it so much easier. All players should take a pride in their appearance and look after their equipment properly.

This attention to detail in dress usually produces a smart team off the field and a successful one on it.

BALLS

Though these are usually provided by the club, it is useful for a player to know something about them. Two-piece balls, those made out of two pieces of leather, swing more than four-piece balls. The cheaper the ball the more damage it is likely to do to a bat since it is usually harder. It is therefore false economy to buy the cheapest ball, as bats may have to be replaced more often. Another indication of the grade of a ball is the size of the individual stitch; the smaller the stitch, the better and more expensive the ball.

The Object of the Game

The primary object or reason for playing cricket or any other similar game must surely be to win and failing this to avoid defeat. To win a cricket match a team or side, usually of eleven players, has to score more runs than their opposition. A run is scored by the two batsmen at

the crease, changing ends and 'making good their ground'— getting behind the batting crease before the fielding side can break the wicket with the ball. The correct call on the toss of a coin allows a captain to decide whether his side shall field or bat first.

Two batsmen always bat together and when a batsman is out another takes his place until ten players are out. The innings of the batting side is then said to be closed or completed. Therefore the task of the batting side is to score as many runs as possible by striking the ball to parts of the field where there are no fielders and secondly to avoid getting out.

A batsman can be out in any of the following ways:

- bowled
- caught
- stumped
- run-out
- leg before wicket
- hit wicket
- hit the ball twice
- handled the ball
- obstructed the field.

The umpires always give the benefit of any doubt to the batsman.

As every member of the team may be called upon to bat, it is to the advantage of the team that everyone should strive to improve his or, since the game is also played by the fair sex, her batting.

The captain of the side batting first may decide his team have scored more runs than the opposition will score and declare his team's innings closed. Alternatively an innings will be closed if the time or number of overs allotted each side to bat or bowl has expired. Cricket has often been likened to war and certainly the handling of the fielding side by a captain has many similarities to it. Since the batsman taking strike tries to protect his wicket from the ball the initial assault on it by the fielding side is the direct attack by a fast bowler. The ball is delivered—bowled—with a straight arm at speeds up to and in excess of 90 miles per hour and aimed to hit the ground in front of the batsman, so that if it is not intercepted by the bat it will break the wicket. This is the primary method of attack—to bowl the batsman out. Some fielders are positioned so that if the batsman does not play the ball down into the ground, or edges it, they can catch the ball before it touches the ground and claim the batsman's wicket.

If this method fails the captain can call on other players to bowl in different ways. Each bowler is only allowed to bowl six or in some competitions eight consecutive balls before the umpire calls over. A different player must then bowl an over from the other wicket. At the completion of an over the batsmen stay at the ends where they are; but the wicketkeeper and fielders change their positions.

Should the fielding side not have much success in getting batsmen out the captain may decide to lay siege to a pair of batsmen by placing his field so that runs are very difficult to obtain. Under these circumstances some batsmen lose patience and play rash strokes; others may be induced to try and make impossible runs, thus getting themselves run out.

Results

Unlike many games there are four possible results for a team in cricket:

A win—the team batting second scores one or more runs than the team which has batted first. The team fielding bowls out the batting side for less runs than the former scored. The time or overs having passed or been bowled and the team batting second not having passed the score of the side which batted first.

Matches can be of two innings each side in which case it is the sum of each team's batting which is taken into the reckoning

A loss—the team not winning as above

A tie—this occurs when the team batting last is all out and the scores are level.

A draw—when a match is unfinished because of weather or the side batting second is not bowled out when time is called in a match, the conditions of which allow for this result.

Some Varieties of the Game

There are many forms of cricket; perhaps the simplest and most competitive is known as single wicket:

SINGLE WICKET

In this game each player bats on his own trying to score as many runs as possible without getting out. The batsman's innings may be limited to a certain number of overs which may all be bowled by one opponent or by several, should they not succeed in getting him out earlier.

There is no fixed number of fielders in this game, but less than six, including the wicketkeeper and bowler, make it very easy for the batsman to score runs: more than 11 is not usually acceptable.

When playing in competitions players are frequently paired against each other and play against each other on a knockout basis, the winner being the one who scores most runs before having his innings terminated.

DOUBLE WICKET

Very similar to single wicket except that a pair of players bat against another pair who bowl alternate overs. An innings is completed when one of the pair is out.

SIX-A-SIDE

This is another game which ensures every player takes a full part. The batting side bat as in full matches, two players together at the wicket. On one being out a fresh batsman comes in to take his place, until all six of the team have batted. When five wickets have fallen the undefeated batsman plays on, taking the strike until all the overs have been bowled or he is out.

Various conditions govern the numbers of overs to be bowled and the maximum number any single bowler may deliver. Even in the briefest match each fielder, excluding the wicketkeeper, must bowl an over if the innings of the batting team lasts long enough. This particular game has been adapted and made suitable for playing indoors, the detailed regulations for which may be obtained from the National Cricket Association.

EIGHT-A-SIDE PAIRS

Developed quite recently to encourage young children to enjoy the game. It has expanded into a national competition at under thirteen years of age with hundreds of teams entering annually.

A pair of batsmen from the batting team bat for a number of overs, usually four or five. No matter how many times the pair are out they continue to bat until all the overs are bowled. They then leave the wicket and another pair from the same team take their places. This continues until all four pairs have batted. The fielding side now have their innings and the winning side is the one which has the best average of runs per wicket lost.

As in six-a-side each member of the fielding side must bowl at least one over with the exception of the wicketkeeper, and no player may bowl more than two overs in a twelve-over game, three overs in a sixteen-over game or four overs in a twenty-over game. The National Cricket Association will be happy to supply detailed instructions concerning the above to anyone requiring them.

ELEVEN-A-SIDE

Anyone associated with cricket expects this number of players to be in a team and this is the usual form of the game when played by adults at club level. A one-day game normally has but one innings per team, the winner being that team which scores the most runs in their innings. In leagues or other competitions the innings of each side may be limited to an agreed number of overs.

In two-, three-, four- or five-day matches, games are of two innings per side and the higher aggregate wins the match. However, draws can result if the weather prevents the teams from completing their innings or if in a game the second innings of the team batting last is incomplete—they are not all out neither have they overtaken the aggregate score of the first team.

No team has to be all out; an innings can be terminated should the captain of the batting side consider he already has more runs scored than he thinks the opposition will make. This is called a declaration and can be made at any time during a game.

(It is not the intention of this publication to explain in detail the laws of Cricket but merely to outline those necessary to understand the basic principles involved.)

Off-side, On-side, Leg-side

The description given to any part of a cricket field or to a player in that area depends on two factors—the end from which the ball is being delivered and the way in which a batsman stands at the wicket. Most batsmen stand on the left of the wicket as they face the bowler, and are called right-handed whilst left-handers stand on the right-hand side. Whichever side the batsman is standing becomes the leg or on-side and conversely the other side of the wicket is called the off-side.

Fielding Positions

Though players specialise in fielding in certain positions only one player, the wicketkeeper, easily recognisable by the fact that he is the only fielder allowed to catch the ball in gloves and protect his legs with pads, can be sure that he will field in the same position all the time. The others may be called upon to bowl or field in any position.

There are an infinite number of places to field and the more commonly named positions are in the diagram. However, the explanation of some terms used may help in understanding how the positions are named.

Deep or *long*—a considerable distance from the batsman taking strike, especially those fielders near the boundary.

Short—applied to those fielders who may be about ten paces or less from the batsman.

Silly—very close to the batsman and rather dangerous fielding positions.

Mid—normally about twenty paces from the striker but can be more than thirty and generally in a fairly narrow arc in front of the batsman.

Fine—usually applied to fielders behind the batsman who have a small angle between themselves and a line through both wickets.

On—in front of the batting crease on the leg-side.

Leg—generally behind the batting crease on the on-side.

Forward—in front of the batsman.

Square—level with the batting crease.

Wide—making a large angle between the fielder and the line of the pitch.

Thus deep-fine-leg is practically on the boundary, making an acute angle between the fielder and the line of the pitch, behind the batsman on the leg-side. Whereas silly-mid-off is extremely close to the batsman, on the off-side and quite straight in front of him.

FIELDING POSITIONS

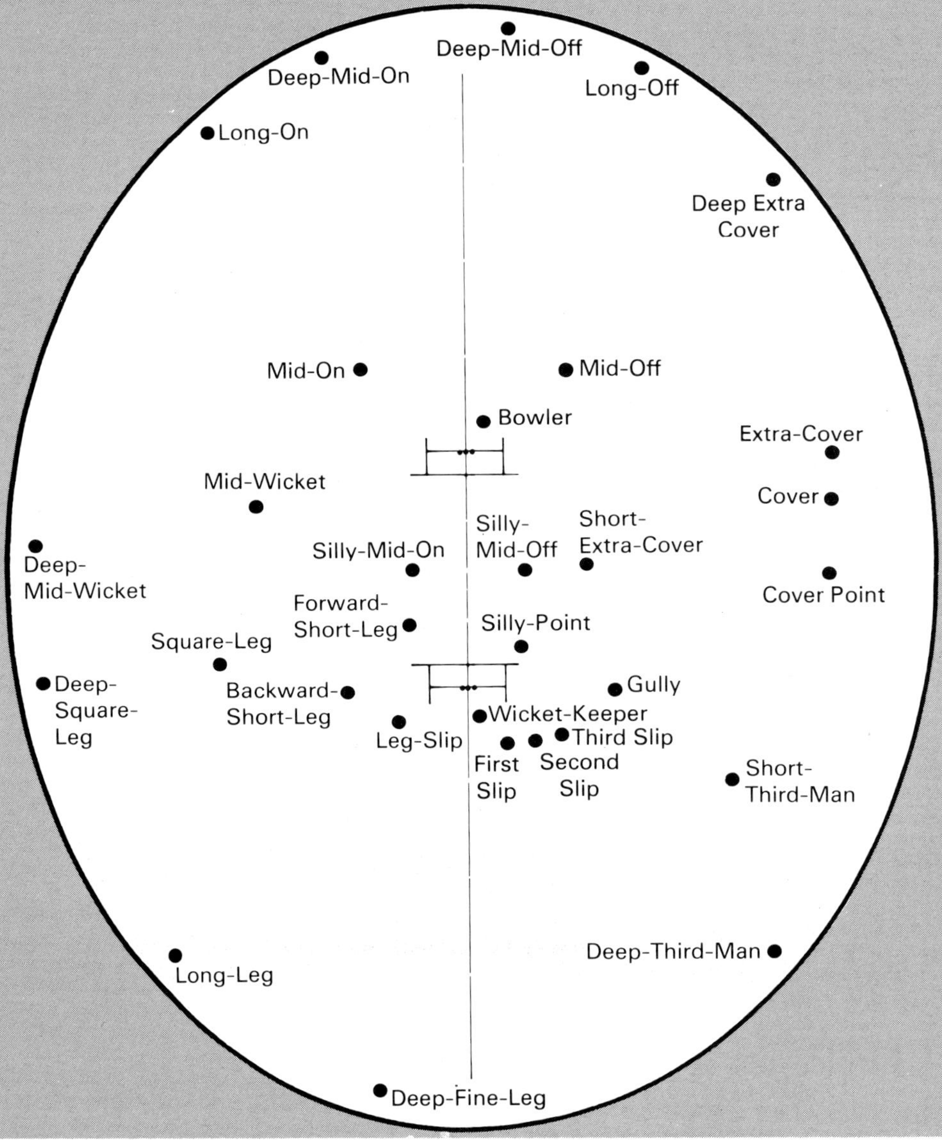

Deep-Mid-Off

Deep-Mid-On

Long-Off

Long-On

Deep Extra Cover

Mid-On

Mid-Off

Bowler

Extra-Cover

Mid-Wicket

Cover

Silly-Mid-On

Silly-Mid-Off

Short-Extra-Cover

Deep-Mid-Wicket

Cover Point

Forward-Short-Leg

Silly-Point

Square-Leg

Deep-Square-Leg

Backward-Short-Leg

Gully

Wicket-Keeper

Leg-Slip

Third Slip

First Slip

Second Slip

Short-Third-Man

Deep-Third-Man

Long-Leg

Deep-Fine-Leg

Bowling

Basic grip

Basic Action

The bowling actions of some great bowlers vary but there are certain fundamentals which are essential. These are:
- a correct grip
- a smooth and economical run-up
- an easy rhythmical and well-balanced delivery, making full use of height and body
- a deliberate and fluent follow-through.

THE BASIC GRIP

1. The ball is held in the fingers, never in the palm of the hand.
2. The seam is vertical between the first and second fingers.
3. Third finger and thumb support the ball underneath.
N.B. Everything that follows is written for a right-arm bowler; for a left-arm reverse 'left' and 'right'.

◄
The fast bowler in action. Note how far the right arm has travelled down and then across the chest, and also note the shoulder pointing down the pitch

1. Start of bound, eyes fixed on line of ball
2. Shoulder turning as left arm is lifted
3. Body almost fully turned prior to landing, right foot passing in front of left

THE RUN-UP AND BOUND

The run-up should be as short as is consistent with the speed at which the bowler is to bowl. Having decided what type of ball he is to bowl, the bowler should accelerate smoothly from the same marked spot for each delivery, building up to a maximum speed only in his last two or three strides before the Bound. In the final stride, he bounds off his left foot, turning sideways in the air to land on his right foot, which should be parallel with the bowling crease. Some bowlers throw the left arm across the body to assist the turning movement of the shoulder and trunk. During the run-up and delivery it is vitally important to watch the batsman and then to fix the eyes on the line of the intended ball or on the spot where it is to pitch.

1. Arms being raised, legs coming through

2. Body leaning away from the batsman; although this bowler bends his front arm at the elbow the upper arm is vertical

3. Still sideways, back arched

THE DELIVERY

Though the delivery must be smooth and rhythmical without hesitations, there are five recognised positions through which a bowler with a good action will pass. They can be summarised as follows:

1. When the body is turning sideways in the air, the left shoulder will be pointing down the pitch, with both arms being raised. The right foot is passing in front of the left and is turning so that it will land parallel to the bowling crease, whilst the bowler is looking down the pitch along the intended line of the ball.

2. The Coil: the right foot has landed parallel to the crease and the weight is on it. The left shoulder and hip are pointing down the pitch with the back slightly arched. The body is leaning away from the batsman,

the delivery. Too long a stride will decrease height; too short a stride may destroy balance.

4. The moment of delivery: The weight of the body is over the front leg, which, having absorbed the impact, is straightening as the right leg begins to come through. The head will be over the left leg or slightly in front of it. The left arm is swinging backwards, close to the body which has turned to face the batsman.

5. The final act of delivery and commencement of the follow-through: both arms have swung down close to the left side of the body and are now pointing behind the bowler. The body has pivoted on the left leg so that the bowler is looking over his right shoulder down the pitch. The right leg is picked up and carried through close to the left.

the left knee is high. The left arm is extended upwards and the bowler is looking down the pitch behind it. The right arm is beginning to swing forward and down to start the delivery swing.

3. When the weight is about to be transferred to the extended front leg, which is about to land

in line with, or slightly to the on-side of, the right leg. The front arm is swinging forwards and down, whilst the right arm is just commencing the upward part of the delivery swing. The body is still sideways to the batsman. The length of the delivery stride is important since it provides the base for

THE FOLLOW-THROUGH

This consists of several strides to absorb the momentum of the action, during which time the bowler should ensure that he does not run down the pitch and damage it in the danger area, i.e. an area contained by an imaginary line 4 ft (1.22 m) from the popping crease and

The follow-through of a fast ▶
bowler. Note how high the left arm
is; the eyes fixed on the ball

First stride of follow-through—the bowler has grounded his right foot clear of danger area

The bowler still watching the ball, head up, continues to move away from the pitch. Had he not done so his left foot would be damaging the pitch on a spinner's length

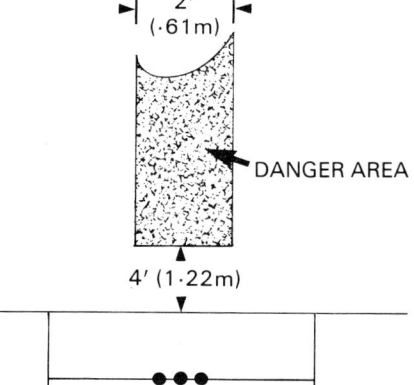

2' (·61m)

DANGER AREA

4' (1·22m)

Danger area to be avoided during follow-through

parallel to it and within two imaginary parallel lines drawn down the pitch from points 1 ft (0.3 m) either side of the middle stump.

COMMON FAULTS

- run-up jerky or too fast
- taking off wrong foot (hopping)
- not turning sideways
- not leaning away from batsman when landing on back foot
- poor use of front arm and not looking behind it with back arched
- not fixing the eyes on target and allowing head to wander incorrect foot placing
- not keeping sideways long enough
- loss of balance and body

- falling away to off-side poor follow-through.

Fast Bowling
TACTICS

Genuine fast bowlers are rare, so the tactics that follow are for very few bowlers. Those who are only fastish should concentrate on learning to make the ball deviate in some way. Generally the opening bowlers are the fastest and have first use of the new ball. This, used correctly, can be a great asset as it comes off the pitch faster and bounces higher when new. Though all bowlers should try to make the batsman play at every delivery, it is even more important for the pace bowler to achieve this, so as not to waste the new ball and run

**Fast bowler
Out-swing**

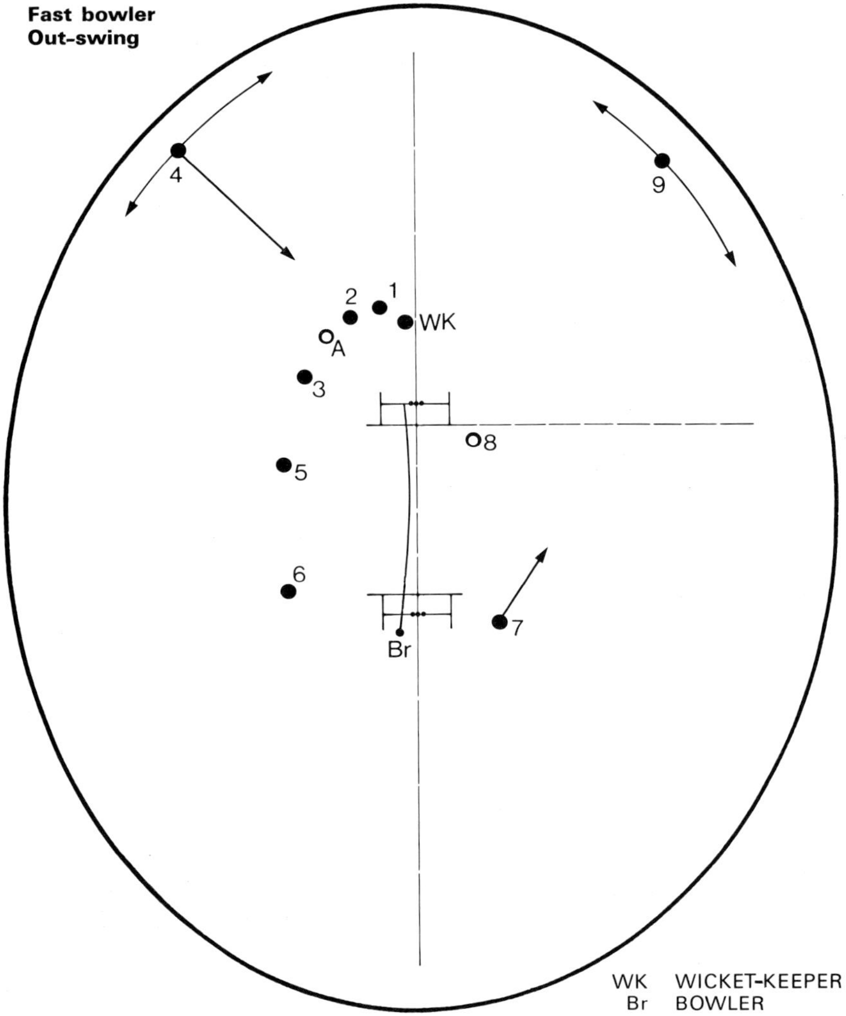

WK

2 1

○A

3

○8

5

6

Br

7

4

9

WK WICKET-KEEPER
Br BOWLER

6/7 on off-side		3/2 on on-side
1 first slip	4 third-man	7 mid-on
2 second slip	5 cover	8 short-square-leg
3 gully	6 mid-off	9 long-leg

When the ball is swinging considerably No. 8 may move to third slip (A),
in which case No. 7 will be wider to cut off singles on the leg side.

down his energy reserves. He is an attacking bowler and should be used in short bursts to maintain maximum speed. Initially he should keep the ball well up to the batsman on the line of middle and off stumps. Provided he has a good action he may obtain a small amount of out-swing and bowling full length allows the ball more time to move in the air. It is also good policy to try to pitch the ball on the seam in order to obtain some deviation after it has pitched, since this presents the batsman with yet another problem. Minor adjustments in the grip of the ball may be necessary for each individual bowler to achieve this.

He, as all bowlers, should try to assess the batsman's basic method of play, e.g. off the front or back foot, and endeavour to bowl such a length as to pre-empt the batsman's favourite strokes. Variation of length is important as this ensures that no batsman can settle into a routine. On pitches which are good or fast the bowler may decide to try to make the batsman play most of his deliveries off the back foot and then slip in the occasional yorker which pitches at the

batsman's feet. This may get underneath the late back lift or through a hurried defensive stroke.

Alternatively, against a player who prefers back-foot strokes, the bowler may bowl a full length trying to get him playing repeatedly off the front foot before bowling a bouncer, i.e. a fast ball that is pitched short enough to bounce at least to chest height. In club cricket this ball should not be used against poor batsmen but as a legitimate weapon against the better ones.

This ball should be bowled from as close to the stumps as possible to make it more difficult for a batsman to get to the off-side of it should he attempt to hook it. Many fast bowlers make the mistake of bowling this (and many other deliveries) from wider out on the crease with the result that the majority of these balls pass harmlessly down the leg-side. The utilisation of this ball should not be overdone. Rather it should be a surprise item which is unleashed occasionally to unsettle batsmen and make them wary of coming on to the front foot too early.

Some fast bowlers who have just been struck for a boundary bowl a bouncer next ball to show their annoyance. This is not the best time as many batsmen expect it. Far better to bowl a yorker as the batsman will almost certainly be ready to play off the back foot instead of the front. Allow the batsman to worry or become apprehensive while he is expecting a bouncer and only bowl it when his complacency has returned. Obviously it is necessary to have a fielder at deep-long-leg if use is going to be made of the bouncer, otherwise the batsman can attempt to hook with impunity.

On dead pitches he must master the art of bowling a good line at middle and off stumps but on a fuller length. Under these circumstances even the really fast bowler can be played comparatively comfortably, so he should learn to vary his pace slightly but without showing obvious alterations to his run-up or delivery. One simple way is to hold the ball nearer the palm of the hand, but if the bowler loses accuracy when attempting this, he should discard the idea and be content to wait for the

batsmen to make a mistake. By accurate bowling and good fielding which deny the batsmen runs pressure is put on them to score, sometimes resulting in run-outs from poorly judged runs attempted by the frustrated players.

Field setting is always a subject that provokes discussion and those diagrams which follow are only basic suggestions for bowlers who bowl accurately against batsmen who play correctly. The diagram on page 26 is for a fast bowler whose stock ball tends to swing away from the batsman who is playing on a fast pitch.

There is a large gap between mid-off and the bowler which encourages the batsman to attempt to drive the ball in that direction. The bowler hopes that if he pitches the ball well up, the batsman will be tempted to try this but that the out-swinger will find the edge of the bat, thus giving a catch to the close fielders on the off-side. Similarly the leg-side is only sparsely guarded to encourage the batsman to hit across the line of the ball.

If the ball swings a great deal, the bowler may prefer to do away with his short-square-leg,

placing him at third slip. Equally, some bowlers prefer to keep the short-leg and move cover to third slip as they feel they can aim more at the middle stump. When wickets are more important than runs third man can be brought up as an extra gully or fourth slip.

The faster the bowler and pitch, the deeper and finer the fielders should be behind the wicket. As the bowler tires, the ball becomes older or the pitch easier paced, so the bowler should ask his captain to set the field slightly squarer, e.g. third man will not have to field so many edges and therefore will move wider (to his right) for balls which have been cut.

Against batsmen who back away to leg, the faster bowler may often be successful if he changes his line so that he is bowling to hit leg stump. It is also good strategy to keep the ball well up to such players since they cannot cut the ball which is close to them.

When bowling against left-handed batsmen the right-arm fast bowler has the same advantages as the left-arm over-the-wicket bowler (see tactics for left-arm seam bowlers). Some bowlers prefer to bowl round the wicket to these batsmen but they usually lose more advantage than they gain by so doing. The two main reasons for bowling round the wicket are: to change the angle of the line of the ball in the hope that this may cause the batsman some difficulty; to make use of any bowler's rough outside the off stump. Usually this is too close to the batsman for fast bowlers to pitch on.

Each bowler must work out for himself the tactics he should use against individual batsmen, but every fast bowler should ensure that he is warmed up before bowling. This not only prevents injury but also ensures that his first few deliveries are not looseners or badly directed, which give the batsman time to adjust to his pace. A good captain assists his bowlers by warning them some time before they are asked to bowl, in order that they can do this, especially after long periods of comparative inactivity in the field.

Practice runs-up at the start of a match will allow the bowler to discover any variations in levels or the need for caution if the footholes are wet, as well as helping to warm him up. However, once play has commenced this is not allowed, but he can jog in from his fielding position to give his sweater to the umpire.

To be successful the fast bowler must be strong, fit, well co-ordinated, aggressive but master of his emotions: not rushing in and bowling wildly on favourable pitches nor giving in easily on less helpful ones. He must be meticulous where maintenance of his equipment is concerned, ensuring that his footwear is correctly spiked for the condition, that socks are comfortable and even making himself rubber heel cushions to prevent bruising on very hard pitches.

Swing Bowling

Bowlers conforming to the basic principles set out previously may find that the ball swings during its flight, i.e. deviates from its original line. This deviation can be assisted by:

- pointing the seam in the direction of the intended swing
- polishing only one side of the ball

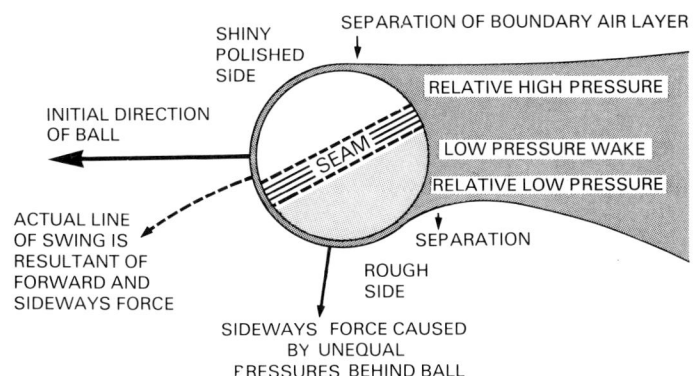

THEORY OF SWING

SEPARATION OF BOUNDARY AIR LAYER

SHINY POLISHED SIDE

RELATIVE HIGH PRESSURE

INITIAL DIRECTION OF BALL

SEAM

LOW PRESSURE WAKE

RELATIVE LOW PRESSURE

ACTUAL LINE OF SWING IS RESULTANT OF FORWARD AND SIDEWAYS FORCE

SEPARATION

ROUGH SIDE

SIDEWAYS FORCE CAUSED BY UNEQUAL PRESSURES BEHIND BALL

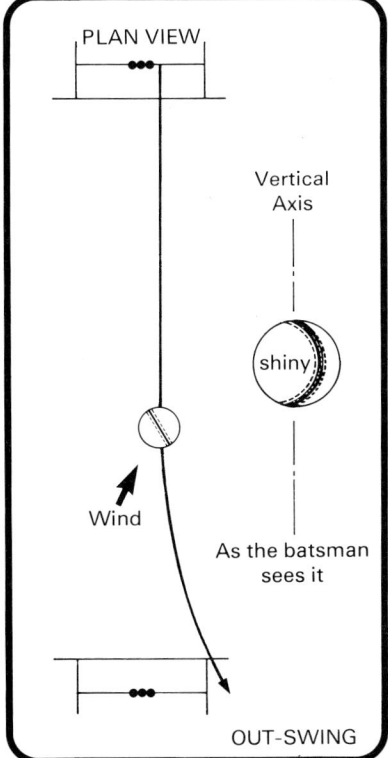

PLAN VIEW

Vertical Axis

shiny

Wind

As the batsman sees it

OUT-SWING

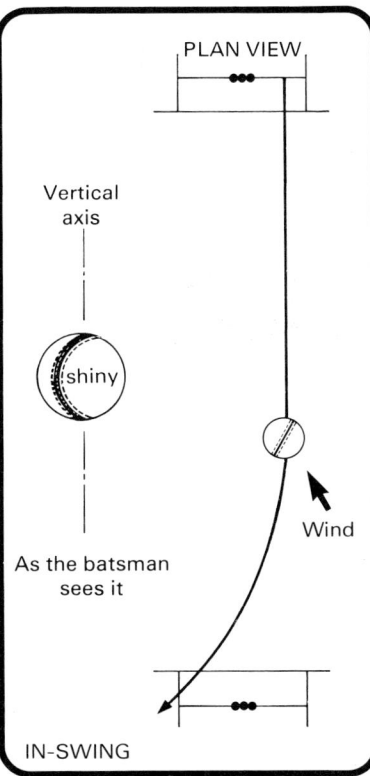

PLAN VIEW

Vertical axis

shiny

Wind

As the batsman sees it

IN-SWING

■ cleaning any dirt out of the seam.

A simple explanation of why a ball swings may help players to understand the modifications of the basic action and grip needed to help a bowler to swing the ball.

As the ball moves through the air, some of it 'sticks' to the ball forming a boundary layer. This layer eventually breaks away from the ball behind it forming a wake. The angled seam and surface roughness delay the separation of this layer on that side, causing an asymmetrical pressure distribution over the rear surface of the ball. The result seen in the diagram makes the ball deviate in flight to the rough side.

THE OUT-SWINGER

This ball, which moves in the air to the off-side, i.e. away from the right-handed batsman, is difficult to play safely when bowled to a full length at the middle and off stumps.

The Grip

The ball is held in the fingers with the seam vertical and pointing to first slip. The inside

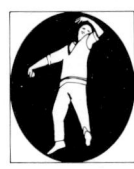

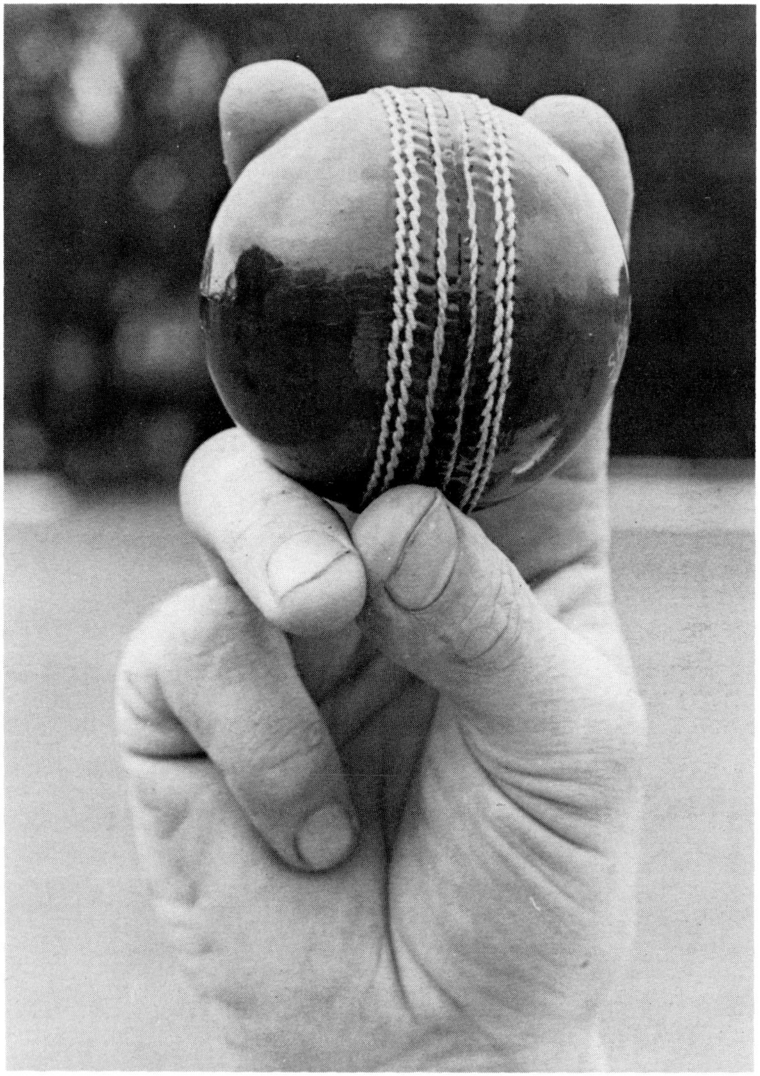

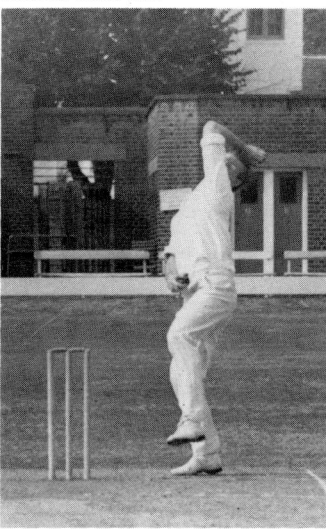

The out-swing grip: seam vertical, pointing at first slip, side of thumb under seam

Good sideways position, looking behind front arm

edge of the thumb will support the ball underneath the seam (see photograph on this page).

The Action

The left shoulder is rotated slightly more than for the normal ball and to assist this the left foot may land slightly to the on-side of the back foot. The ball is delivered with the arm high, the fingers remaining behind the ball as long as possible and the wrist held a little stiffer than normally. A good body pivot and strong follow-through with the right arm swinging past the left thigh complete the action.

Left foot moving slightly across towards on-side

Toes of left foot pointing to fine leg, body just starting to pivot

High delivery, fingers behind the ball

Good follow-through with right arm swinging past left thigh

Tactics

The medium-pace bowler's great virtue should be his ability to maintain good length and direction on plumb pitches. When asked to bowl under these conditions his main method of attack will be to frustrate the batsmen by preventing them from scoring. Many people think this is negative cricket, but this is not so if the bowler's target is the stumps.

The length the bowler should attempt to pitch is that which causes the greatest uncertainty in a batsman's mind as to whether to play forward or back. This varies from day to day according to the condition of the pitch, ball, pace and trajectory of each delivery. By watching the batsman play each ball the intelligent bowler quickly learns where this place is. A rough guide is given by the position of the ball on the bat when it is struck. If it strikes the bat in a forward stroke above half way up the blade, the batsman has probably misjudged the length. Similarly if he is playing back to a ball bouncing normally and this fails to reach knee height or induces a very hurried stroke, the batsman will have been deceived again by a good-length delivery. Faced with such bowling directed at the middle and off stumps together with the field set as for medium-pace with an old ball, the batsmen have to take risks and probably pay the penalty. However, when time is on the the side of the batsmen the bowler has to attack them by setting an attacking field as for medium-pace out-swing, and vary his bowling more. He can do this by altering his delivery position on the crease, changing the pace, adopting a different grip or by bowling a different type of ball, e.g. an off-cutter

**Medium-pace
bowler
Out-swing**

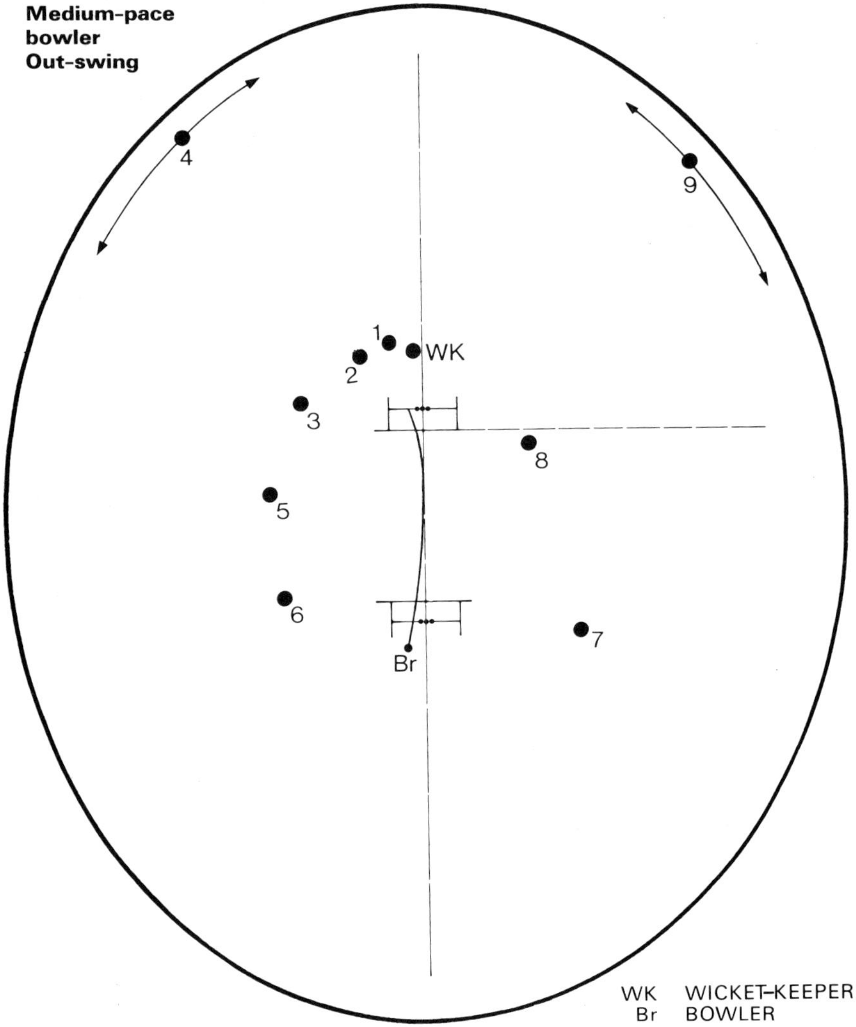

1
2
WK
3
8
5
6
Br
7
4
9

WK   WICKET–KEEPER
Br   BOWLER

(see page 39).
However, when conditions are
favourable for swing this
bowler really comes into his
own. Swing is not sufficient on
its own to obtain the wickets of
good batsmen, it merely delays
their strokes. It must be allied
with good length and direction.
The closer to the stumps the
bowler can deliver, the less the
ball has to swing to beat the
bat. This type of bowler, usually
with a high action, almost
invariably appears to produce
late swing whereas those with
low actions, i.e. 'slingers', seem
to develop early swing. (This
may only be an optical illusion
caused by the initial direction of
the ball.) Obviously the
apparent late swing is more
difficult to play and bowlers
should endeavour to obtain it.
A change of pace may also alter
the amount of swing obtained,
so the medium-pacer should
vary his speed to obtain greater
or lesser degrees of swing.
The primary object of the out-
swing bowler is to beat the bat
on the off-side; hence the
preponderance of fielders on
that side of the wicket. To do
this the bowler must aim at the
middle and off stumps making
allowances for the swing. Some

6 on off-side		3 on on-side
1 first slip	4 third-man	7 mid-on
2 second slip	5 cover	8 square-leg
3 gully	6 mid-off	9 long-leg

balls swing a great deal more than others, and when using such a ball, the bowler may have to alter his grip, position on the crease or his point of aim.

The easiest is probably to aim at the batsmen's pads as this requires no change of grip or run-up. It is also a difficult ball to play when bowled to a full length with a late swing moving the ball back towards the off-side. A similar problem is set to batsmen if the bowler bowls from wider out on the crease as this allows the bowler to maintain the same degree of change in direction but the ball will still be capable of hitting the stumps.

Against batsmen who favour playing to leg, the out-swinger is very useful as they frequently hit across the line. The bowler should maintain his line and field setting to encourage the making of such risky strokes. However, should a batsman be repeatedly successful the bowler must change his line or strengthen the on-side field. Many English players tend to play off the front foot too frequently. By keeping the ball well up a bowler may lull a batsman into a false sense of

security and get him playing rather a long way in front of his pads. If the out-swing bowler has learned to bowl the off-cutter this is the time to use it. It may bowl the batsman 'through-the-gate', the gap between the bat and pad, or the slight difference in pace may induce a catch in front of the wicket.

To be successful a medium-pace bowler must have concentration and determination, for he will be expected to bowl for long spells. An even temperament is also an asset which will help him through those spells when nothing goes right. Equally it prevents him from relaxing his efforts when fortune smiles on him.

Finally he should be prepared to alter his field placing or method of attack as circumstances dictate but always be looking for new ways in which to attack the batsmen.

THE IN-SWINGER

This is a ball which moves during flight in towards the batsman and to the leg-side. The bowler should aim to pitch the ball on or just outside the off stump.

The in-swing grip: seam vertical, pointing to fine leg, ball of thumb under seam, fingers close together on top

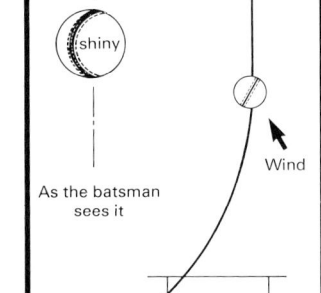

PLAN VIEW

Vertical axis

shiny

Wind

As the batsman sees it

IN-SWING

The Grip

The ball is held with the seam vertical and pointing to fine-leg, with first and second fingers close together either side of the seam. The ball of the thumb will be under the seam.

The Action

This differs from the basic action in that the front foot is placed farther to the off-side and the eyes are looking at the batsman from inside the front arm. As a result the bowler presents more of his chest to the batsman prior to delivery and thus his left side is not used to the full. The ball is delivered from as high as possible but in the follow-through the arm may come down the right side of the body.

Tactics

For many players this is an easy ball to bowl but it demands a great deal of accuracy to be effective.

The ball must be aimed so that, after it pitches, it is going to hit the wickets. To do this it must pitch on the off stump or outside it. Since in-swing

bowlers generally tend to bowl from wider on the crease than out-swing bowlers, balls pitching on the stumps pass harmlessly down the leg-side. The bowler should try to keep the batsman playing off the front foot by keeping the ball well up to him. Variation of pace may enable the ball to bowl the batsman 'through the gate', if he is hurried into a poorly executed forward stroke.

As can be seen from the diagram (page 37) when the field is set for an in-swing bowler, the off-side has many gaps in it. This may encourage the batsman to try to hit the ball through them and induce a mistake. However, should the batsman repeatedly succeed in doing this, the bowler must pitch closer to the line of the off stump or strengthen the off-side.

In-swing bowlers should always try to deliver the ball from as high a position as possible to produce bounce on good firm pitches. The ball which bounces higher than the batsman anticipates is very dangerous and may result in a catch for the close fielder.

An alternative ball that the in-swing bowler should try to develop is the leg-cutter. (see page 39). This is an extremely

6. Bowler moving off the pitch as the ball moves in to the batsman

Medium-pace bowler In-swing

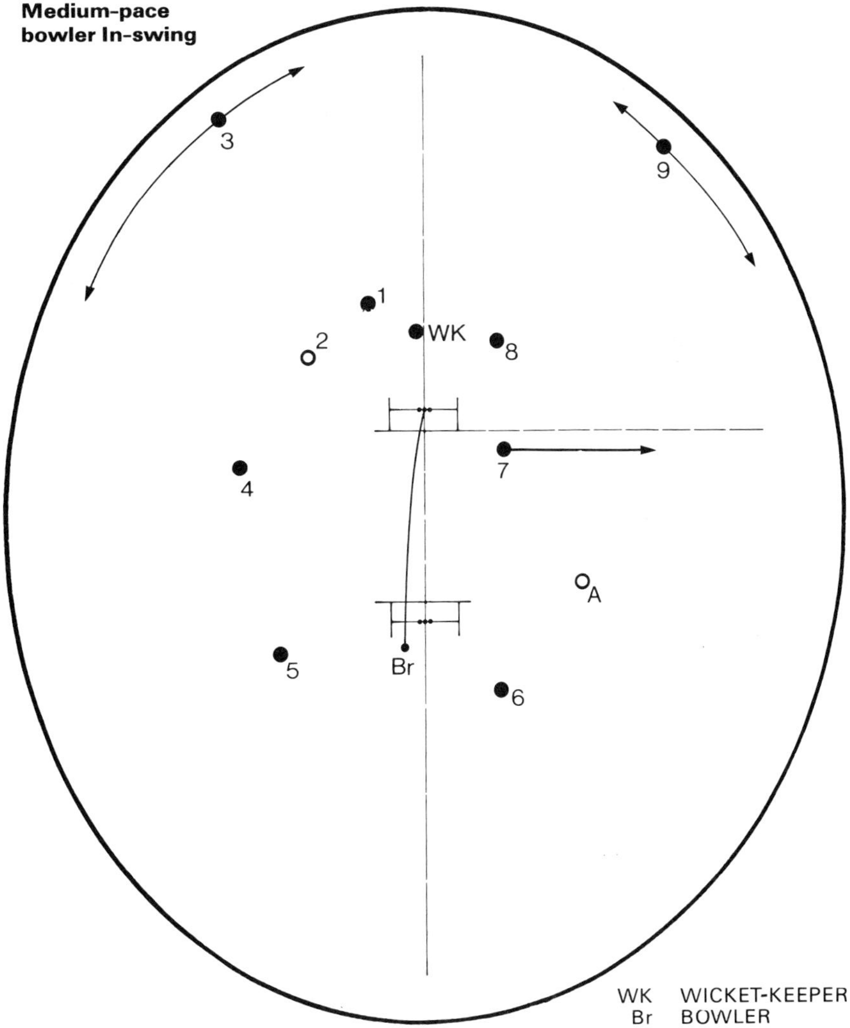

3

9

1

2 ●WK 8

4

7

5   Br   6

A

WK WICKET-KEEPER
Br BOWLER

5/4 on off-side		4/5 on on-side	
1 slip	4 cover	6 mid-on	8 leg-slip
2 gully	5 mid-off	7 square-leg	9 long-leg
3 third-man			

Some bowlers may prefer to have No. 2 on the leg-side (A). When there is little swing No. 7 will drop back to save the single.

difficult ball to play when bowled well and even more so if the batsman was expecting the ball to swing in to him. However, if the bowler has fielders in the short-leg position he should only bowl it if he can pitch it with a good degree of accuracy.
There are times when this bowler may find it advantageous to bowl from round the wicket, especially

A left-arm pace bowler. Note his eyes looking down the pitch and the ball held in the fingers ◀

when the ball is swinging a great deal and left-handed batsmen are at the crease. Even then he must remember that in-swing bowlers must try to ensure that every ball should be aimed to hit the stumps and that those outside leg pose more problems to the wicketkeeper than to the batsman.

LEFT-ARM SEAM BOWLING

These bowlers, whether fast or medium-pace, should bowl mostly from over the wicket. This enables them to bowl across the right-handed batsman aiming at middle and off stumps. Because of the direction of the ball, some batsmen may play inside the line giving chances of catches on the off-side. Since the natural swing of the left-arm bowler is in to the right-hander, there is always the possibility of bowling batsmen through the gate, if they become too concerned about the ball leaving them.
Field setting can be difficult, so each bowler must decide whether his primary method of attack is the in-swinger or the ball slanted across the batsman and set the field accordingly.

Cutters

THE OFF-CUTTER

This ball is usually delivered by an out-swing bowler and moves off the pitch into the batsman.

The Grip

The first finger lies on top of the seam, which is vertical and pointing to the batsman, with the second finger fairly close to it. The ball is supported by the thumb pressed on the seam from underneath.

The Action

The first finger pulls down on the seam imparting a clockwise spin to the ball as it is released and the hand rotates slightly.

THE LEG-CUTTER

A very dangerous ball when bowled well—usually by an in-swing bowler—which should pitch on the middle or middle and off stumps and move towards the off-side.

The Grip

The ball is held with the second finger along the seam, the first finger comfortably placed from it and the thumb underneath.

The grip for the off-cutter

The grip for the leg-cutter

The Action
As the ball is delivered, the second finger pulls down across the seam, the thumb pushes and the wrist rotates slightly, imparting an anti-clockwise spin to the ball. Again, a high delivery and good follow-through are important.

Spin Bowling
All would-be spin bowlers should learn to spin the ball and then try to develop length and direction, not vice versa. On good pitches the spinner will have to rely on flight, good length and direction. On some pitches the quicker the spinner can 'push the ball through' without losing accuracy and still make it turn, the better will be his results.

THE OFF-SPINNER
This ball moves off the pitch into the batsman as a result of clockwise spin imparted mainly by the fingers.

The Grip
The ball is gripped between the first and second fingers with the seam at right-angles to them.

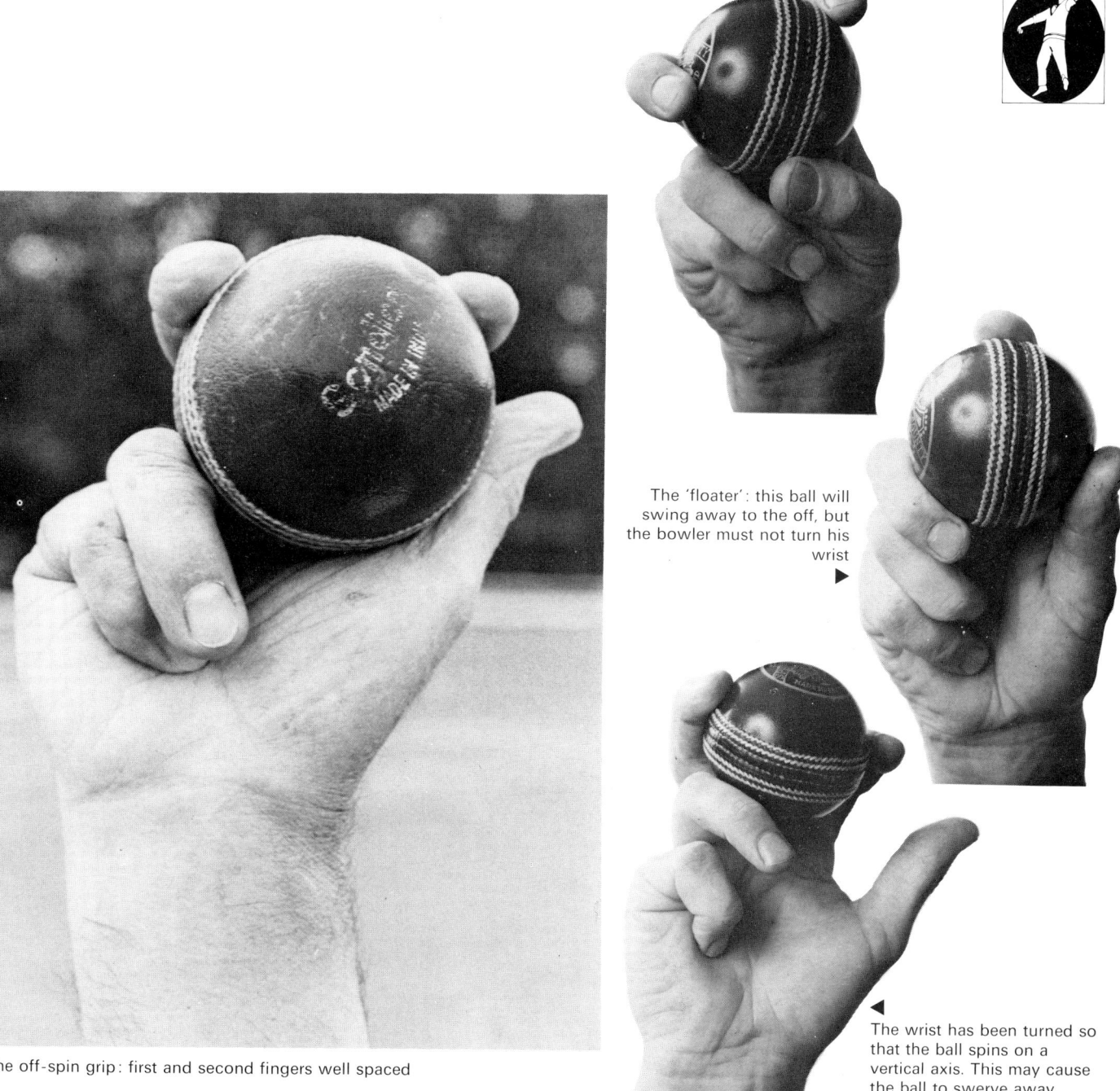

An alternative grip for an off-spinner ▶

The 'floater': this ball will swing away to the off, but the bowler must not turn his wrist ▶

◀ The wrist has been turned so that the ball spins on a vertical axis. This may cause the ball to swerve away

The off-spin grip: first and second fingers well spaced

Good sideways position, palm of bowling hand facing upwards

High delivery position, front leg straight, ball released when the arm is level with the head

Hand continuing to turn after release

Follow-through of arm past left thigh

The farther these two fingers can be spaced apart with comfort, the greater will be the spin imparted. The top joint of the first finger should be on the seam. Some adults and children with small fingers may find this difficult and an alternative is to place the pad of the first finger on the seam. The thumb plays no part at all in this delivery.

The Action

The off-spin bowler needs a good basic action and body pivot. The wrist is bent towards the thumb side, i.e. cocked, so that at the bottom of the delivery swing the palm is facing upwards. As the ball is delivered, the fingers and wrist twist in a clockwise direction and then continue down across the body into the follow-through position. To obtain maximum height, off-spinners use a comparatively short delivery stride, a high arm action and a straight front leg. The ball is released when the left side is braced and the arm is level with the head.

Tactics

First and foremost he is a spin bowler and should concentrate on trying to spin the ball. On pitches that are not helpful the bowler should bowl over the wicket directing his attack at or just outside the off stump. With the field set as in the first diagram on page 43 the batsman is forced to take risks to score if he tries to avoid hitting the ball into the area covered by the fielders. Should the batsman succeed in piercing the off-side field regularly, the bowler may decide to strengthen it by bringing an on-side fielder across or by changing his direction of attack to the middle and off stumps.

The bowler should also be able to deceive the batsman by

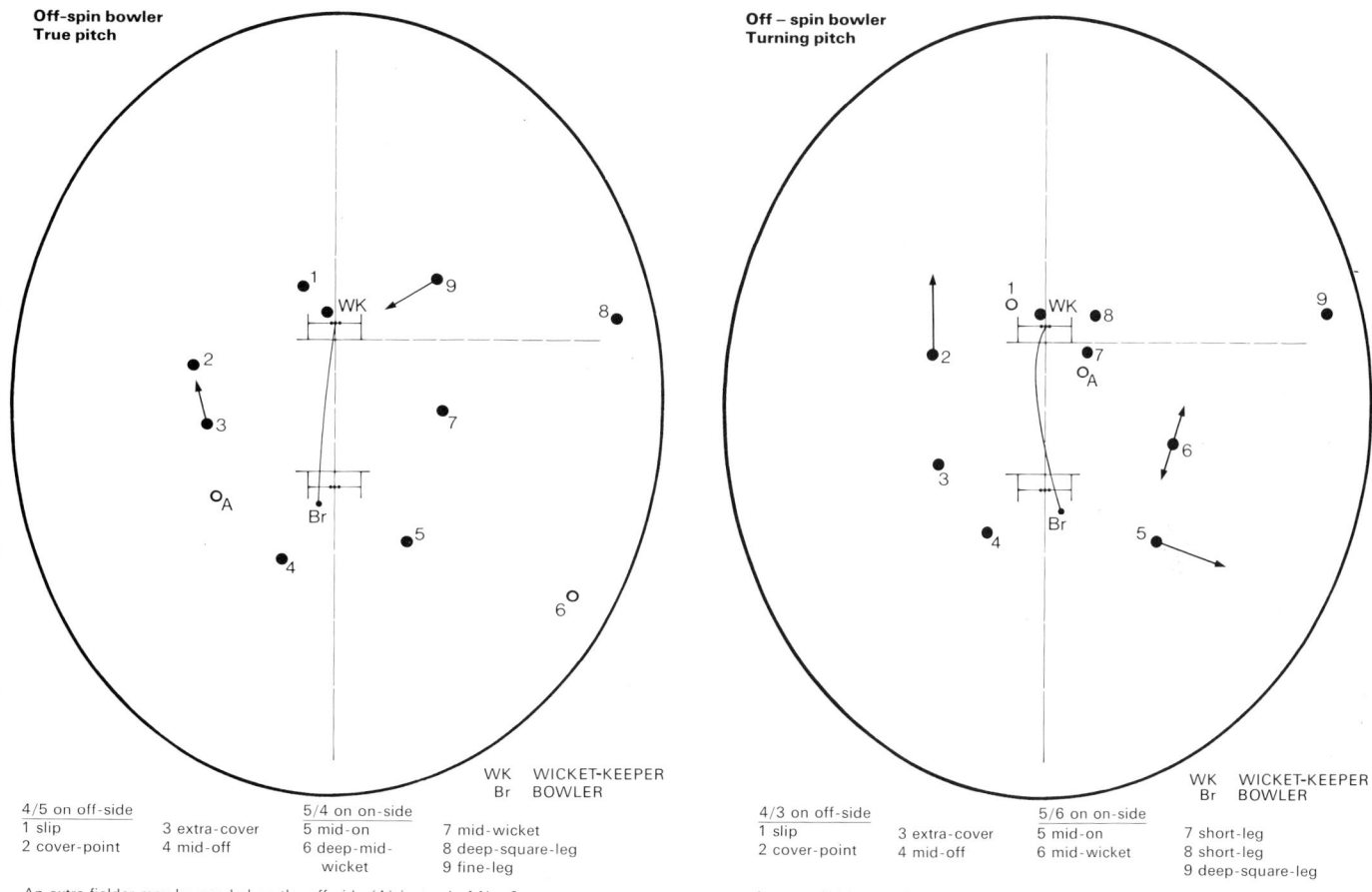

**Off-spin bowler
True pitch**

**Off – spin bowler
Turning pitch**

WK   WICKET-KEEPER
Br   BOWLER

4/5 on off-side		5/4 on on-side	
1 slip	3 extra-cover	5 mid-on	7 mid-wicket
2 cover-point	4 mid-off	6 deep-mid-wicket	8 deep-square-leg
			9 fine-leg

An extra fielder may be needed on the off-side (A) instead of No. 6 depending on the bowler's line of attack and on the batsman.

WK   WICKET-KEEPER
Br   BOWLER

4/3 on off-side		5/6 on on-side	
1 slip	3 extra-cover	5 mid-on	7 short-leg
2 cover-point	4 mid-off	6 mid-wicket	8 short-leg
			9 deep-square-leg

An extra fielder may be needed on the leg-side (A) instead of No. 1 depending on the degree of turn and on the batsman.

flighting the ball. One way to achieve this is to release the ball fractionally earlier or later than for a normal delivery. If the ball is released early it has a high trajectory and the batsman may be deceived into playing too early. Conversely, a later release with perhaps a slightly quicker arm swing may convince the batsman that the ball will be short, which in turn could produce a hurried or fatal stroke.

Using the width of the crease, when bowling on good pitches, is also a valid method of providing more problems for the batsman. Although normally the off-spin bowler's arm should be as high as possible at the moment of release, variations in its height also alter the line of the ball.

On occasions a well-disguised out-swinger may be tried. Some bowlers use a special grip which is not unlike the off-spin grip when viewed from a distance. This is sometimes called a 'floater'. Yet another variation is to alter the angle of the wrist at the moment of delivery, so that the side of the hand faces the batsman. Spin is still imparted to the ball but it revolves around a vertical axis and the ball may swerve in the air to the off-side.

However, the bowler should not employ too many variations unless he is sure that his line

and length will not suffer.
Generally the better the pitch,
the more he must try to beat the
batsman in the air, utilising a
slightly slower pace than usual
for the majority of deliveries.
Should the batsman still have
the better of the encounter, the
spinner will have to attack the
middle and leg stumps with
quicker balls having flat
trajectories. In turn this may
mean an adjustment to the field.
Under favourable conditions,
when the ball is turning, he
should bowl round the wicket
and particularly at a left-handed
batsman. The ball must be
pitched right up to the batsman
to keep him on the front foot.
Bowling short or allowing the
batsman to play off the back
foot gives him more time to
watch the ball, and it is very easy
to score from, as well as
destroying the confidence of the
close catchers.
Many spinners try to spin the
ball too much on turning
pitches, frequently pulling the
ball down so it pitches short, or
turning it, so that the batsman
need not offer a stroke.
Accuracy is vital and the bowler
should try to bowl in a relaxed
manner, not tense or trying too
hard.

The leg-break as the bowler sees it, the ball cupped in well-spaced fingers

The same grip seen from behind: the third finger bent parallel with the seams. This bowler has small fingers, hence the top joint of the second finger is not quite on the seam

When the pitch is a slow turner, the ball must be bowled quicker than on fast-turning pitches, to hasten the batsman's stroke and rob him of thinking time. Even under these favourable bowling conditions there are occasions when the bowler may have to vary the amount of spin he imparts to defeat a good player.

This can be achieved, as stated earlier, by altering the spacing of the fingers or by altering the position of the seam so that it has less chance of hitting the ground.

Finally the off-spinner should look after the ball. This means cleaning all mud out of the seam and polishing one side of the ball as this will not only assist him but also the other bowlers in his team.

THE LEG-BREAK, GOOGLY AND TOP-SPINNER

Since these three deliveries are all part of a leg-spin bowler's armoury and the grip is the same, they can be explained in the same section.

The leg-break is a ball which is

Note left foot about to land wider for googly

Note more open position of coil for googly

Fingers on top of ball for leg-break, underneath for googly

Leg-break sequence

Googly sequence

Note arm does not roll over in leg-break; in the googly the palm faces square leg

Note slightly different follow-through of bowling arm

spun in an anti-clockwise direction so that when it pitches it moves from leg to off: the googly is bowled with virtually the same action but spins from off to leg; the top-spinner is bowled so that it spins down the pitch towards the batsman.

The Grip

The ball is placed in a cup formed by the first two fingers, which are spaced comfortably apart, and the base of the thumb. The third finger is bent parallel with the seam which is at right-angles to and passes under the top joints of the first and second fingers. (See page 45.)

Action for the Leg-Break

A good basic action will assist the leg-break bowler, but it is the action of the wrist and fingers which are different. Initially the wrist is bent forward towards the forearm and then rotated outwards, i.e. little finger leading. Then as the bowling arm approaches its highest point the wrist flips forward towards the batsman, the third finger flicking outwards and imparting the anti-clockwise spin to the ball. The palm

starts by facing fine-leg and is facing downwards as the ball is released. The follow-through as usual is past the left thigh.

Action for the Googly

Though similar to the leg-break, the action of the wrist is different in that it rotates earlier so that the back of the wrist leads and the palm faces away from the batsman. The fingers work as for the leg-break but because of the position of the hand the ball can be felt leaving it over the third and little fingers, thus imparting off-spin. To allow for the extra rotation of the wrist most bowlers allow the front foot to splay slightly to the off-side. There is a tendency to deliver 'open chested' with a consequent dropping of the left shoulder and slightly higher swing of the bowling arm. During the follow-through, the bowling arm points down the pitch with the palm usually facing the square-leg area.

Action for the Top-Spinner

The top-spinner is bowled by rotating the wrist slightly earlier than for the leg-break and the spin is imparted down the line of the flight and not

**Leg-spin bowler
True pitch**

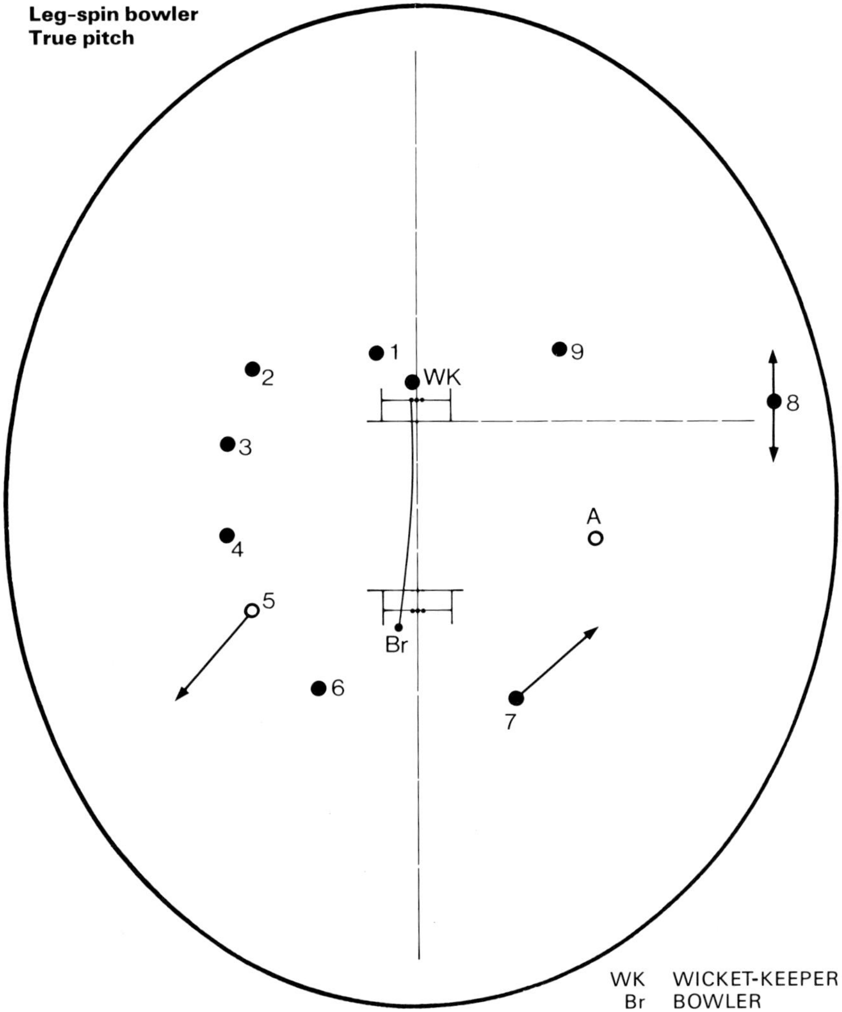

WK WICKET-KEEPER
Br BOWLER

6/5 on off-side		3/4 on on-side
1 slip		7 mid-on
2 short-third-man	4 extra-cover	8 deep-square-leg
3 cover	5 deep-extra-cover	9 short-fine-leg
	6 mid-off	

An extra fielder may be needed at mid-wicket (A) instead of No. 5 depending on the batsman or the accuracy of the bowler.

**Leg-spin bowler
Turning pitch**

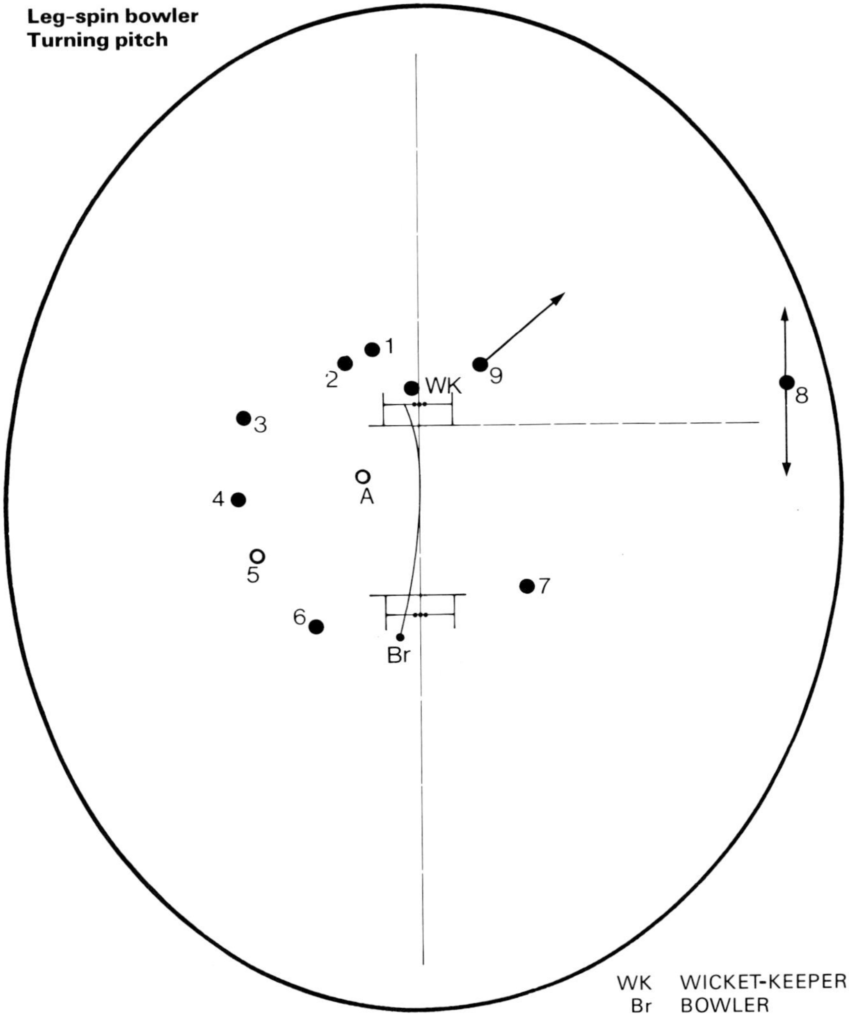

1
2
●3
4 ●
5
6 ●
Br

WK
A
7 ●
9
8

WK   WICKET-KEEPER
Br   BOWLER

6 on off-side		3 on on-side
1 first-slip	4 cover	7 mid-on
2 second-slip	5 extra-cover	8 deep-square-leg
3 short-third-man	6 mid-off	9 leg-slip

Against a defensive batsman the bowler may prefer a silly mid-off (A)
instead of No. 5.

towards the slips. Few bowlers
have sufficient control to
ensure the ball does not deviate
to leg or off after pitching.

Tactics for the Leg-Break Bowler

Almost without exception leg-
break bowlers are attacking
bowlers and should bowl from
over the wicket. Because the
degree of control necessary to
pitch accurately is so fine, few
have ever been able to bowl
defensively. Bearing this in
mind, a leg-break bowler should
keep the ball well up to the
batsman, inviting the drive, but
varying his line according to
the deviation obtained after
pitching. Since he cannot
be awarded an lbw decision
if he pitches outside the line
of the leg stump, it is of
paramount importance to bowl
accurately at the stumps. On the
very odd occasion, perhaps to a
left-handed batsman, he might
bowl round the wicket in an
attempt to gain some advantage
from the bowler's rough outside
the left-hander's off stump.
The faster and truer the pitch,
the more he must rely on
variations of flight to lure the
batsman into errors. Under

49

► One of the
few
leg-spinners
in English
cricket
photographed
in position 3

these conditions, with his better fielders in the covers, he attacks the off stump so that the batsman plays the ball into the packed off-side field with little chance of piercing it. The lightly defended leg-side may tempt the batsman to hit across the line of the ball and against the spin to produce a possible catch in the covers.

The use of the googly at these times may prove profitable but it should not be employed too frequently. Over-bowling of the googly may inhibit the leg-break action completely.

It should be bowled so that if the batsman misreads it, the ball will break the wicket. In other words it has to pitch no farther to leg than the off stump and preferably outside it so that any turn obtained does not carry the ball completely across the stumps. If the bowler has previously been attacking the stumps with his leg-breaks and then pitches the ball well outside the off stump, a good batsman would immediately suspect a googly and be very wary of playing that ball as a leg-break. The bowler should lead up to it by bowling a series of leg-breaks pitching slightly more to the off-side

before slipping in the googly. Against an experienced batsman or one who knows that the bowler can bowl a googly, it may be better to bowl no googlies at all in the early overs of a spell. Then, because the batsman expects one to be bowled, he may mistake an orthodox leg-break for a googly, offering the chance of a catch at the wicket or in the slips. A similar ploy against a batsman who is not familiar with the bowler is to bowl the googly at him quite early in his innings. If he reads it correctly he has the same dilemma as previously described; if he fails to recognise it the bowler may be rewarded with a wicket.

When a pitch assists him by taking spin accuracy is essential. It is better to over-pitch slightly than to under-pitch. If the pitch is slow then he should try to 'push the ball through' to ensure that the batsman has the minimum of time to watch the ball on to the bat.

Should he be able to bowl the top-spinner, its best use is on the faster pitch against a batsman who is trying to play the majority of deliveries off the back foot. A slight

misjudgement of length by the batsman and the slightly quicker movement off the pitch by the ball may reward the bowler with a wicket.

The bowler and his captain must be prepared to accept that runs can be scored quite freely from most leg-break bowlers: the important fact is his wicket-taking record or potential.

Finally he must be prepared to adapt his field and method of attack to combat the particular type of stroke play that each batsman employs.

Left-Arm Spin Bowling

The left-arm bowler who spins the ball from leg to off should follow the advice set out previously for the grip and action as for the off-spin bowler. He too must rely on flight and variation of pace when bowling on good pitches, directing his attack at the off stump or just outside, and delivering the ball usually from round the wicket but as close to the stumps as possible. Against left-handed batsmen he may bowl from over the wicket, particularly if there is any bowler's rough near the line of

A left-arm spinner at the crease. ▶ Note the high front arm, eyes looking over the shoulder and back foot parallel to the bowling crease

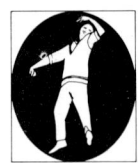

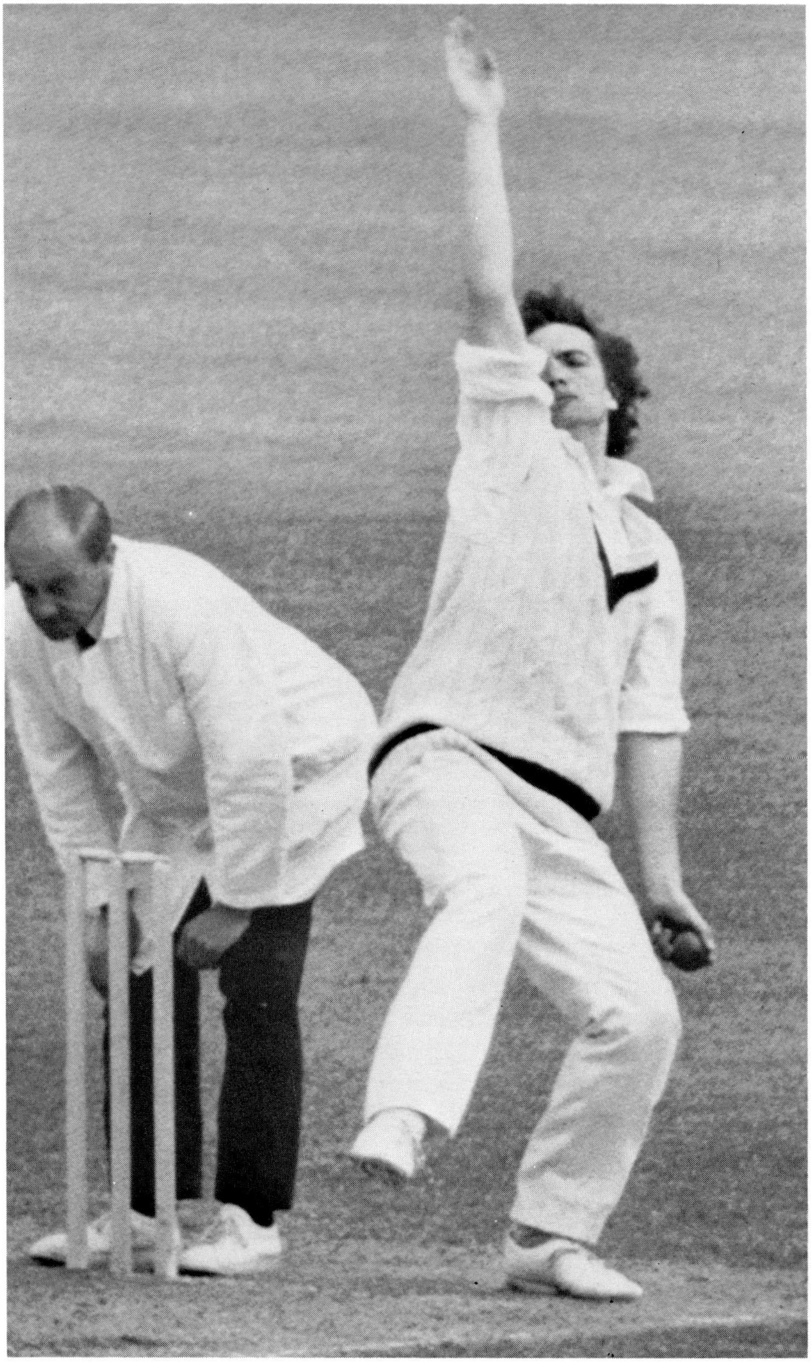

the off stump.
On turning pitches he must bowl round the wicket, keeping the ball well up to the batsman on the line of the middle stump. He may not have to spin the ball quite so much: accuracy is all-important. The more the ball is turning, the wider slip and gulley may have to field.
The most infrequently met bowler is the left-arm wrist-spinner who bowls the 'Chinaman', i.e. an off-spinner to a right-handed-batsman. Because he has the same degree of difficulty in pitching a good length and direction as a leg-spin bowler he may be expensive at times. However, since batsmen so seldom play against such bowling he may achieve considerable success. His action and flight are in all ways similar to the leg-spin bowler but he should attack the off stump with a fairly strong leg-side field.

Some Laws Affecting Bowlers

All bowlers should be fully aware of the laws which apply to them, especially those concerning no-balls, since the latter dictates how and from

Left-arm slow bowler
True pitch

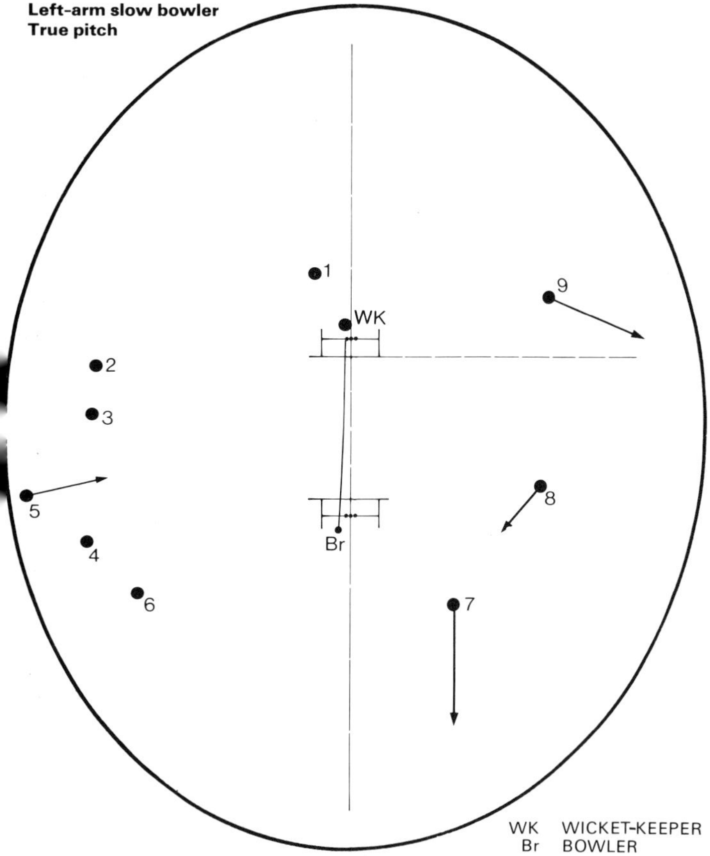

WK

Br

Left-arm slow bowler
Turning pitch

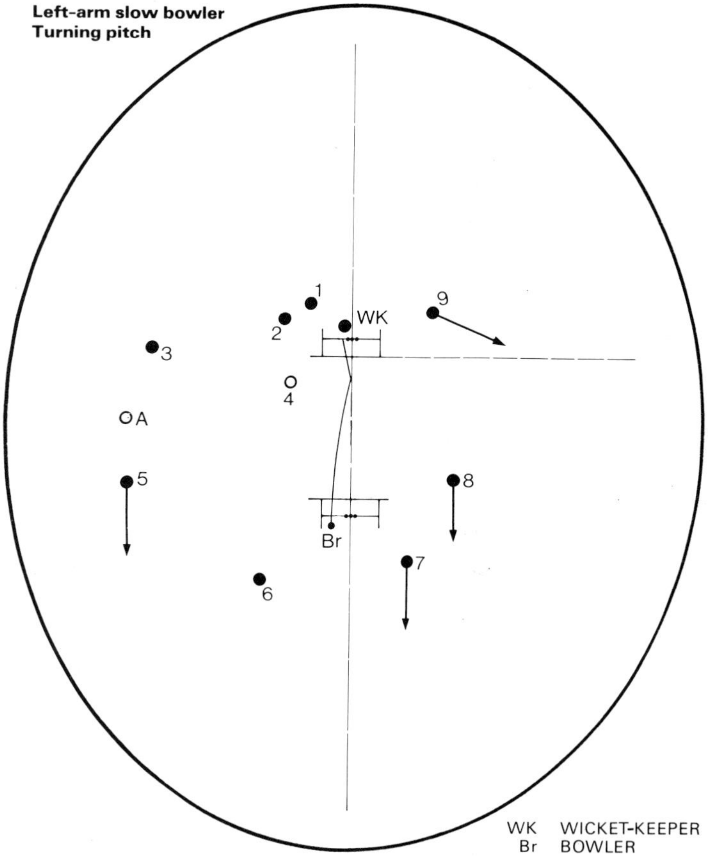

WK

O A

Br

WK   WICKET-KEEPER
Br   BOWLER

6 on off-side   3 on on-side
1 slip   4 extra-cover   7 mid-on
2 square-cover-point 5 deep-extra-cover   8 mid-wicket
3 cover-point   6 deep-mid-off   9 short-fine-leg
The exact position of the leg-side field will depend on the type of
batsman.

WK   WICKET-KEEPER
Br   BOWLER

6 on off-side   3 on on-side
1 first slip   4 silly-mid-off   7 mid-on
2 second slip   5 cover   8 mid-wicket
3 short-third-man   6 mid-off   9 backward short-
                                              leg

Against an attacking batsman an extra fielder will be needed in
the covers (A) instead of No. 4. The position of the leg-side field
will also depend on the batsman.

where the ball is released. The law states that during the delivery stride some part of the bowler's front foot must be behind the popping crease though not necessarily grounded. The back foot must land within the return crease or its forward extension. It must not be grounded on or outside this crease, although if part of the foot is over the crease as long as it is not grounded this would not constitute a no-ball. Bowlers should practise bowling whenever possible with the correct crease markings, so that they, their coach or some other person can check that they are conforming to the laws. Failure to do this may lead to the bowling of no-balls in matches.

Players as well as coaches should look critically at bowlers' actions during practice to ensure that the ball is not jerked or thrown. Any bowler who is beginning to develop such faults must be informed immediately, so that he can try to eradicate them before they become habitual.

No batsman is out until such time as the umpire has given this decision following an appeal. Frivolous and unnecessary appeals only annoy umpires, players and spectators; therefore the bowler should curb his exuberance and only make an enquiry following some thought. A thorough study of the lbw laws not only cuts down the number of appeals but also assists a bowler by teaching him where he must pitch the ball to have an appeal upheld.

There are also laws governing what a player may do with the ball. Polishing the ball, provided no agents (oils, grease, etc.) are used, is allowed, but a player may not deliberately roughen the ball by rubbing it on the ground.

THE NO-BALL LAW FOOT POSITIONS FOR BOWLERS

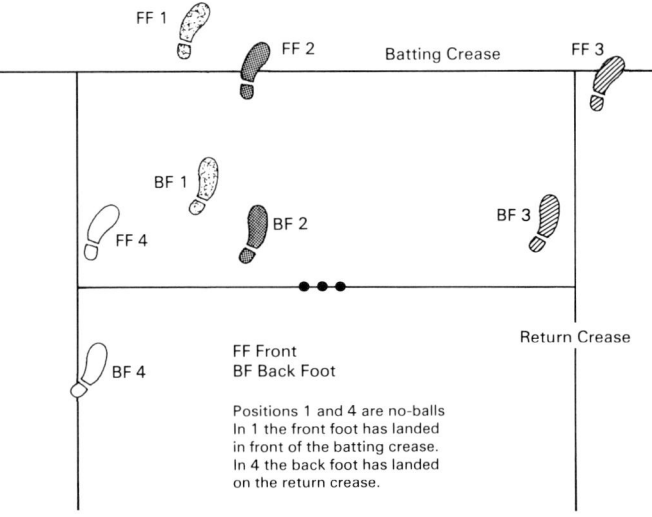

FF 1
FF 2   Batting Crease   FF 3
BF 1
FF 4   BF 2   BF 3
BF 4
FF Front
BF Back Foot
Return Crease

Positions 1 and 4 are no-balls
In 1 the front foot has landed
in front of the batting crease.
In 4 the back foot has landed
on the return crease.

Fielding

Principles

Nothing more than good fielding makes for the enjoyment of cricket and there is no excuse for any member of a team not to improve his fielding through endeavour and enthusiasm. Anyone who has batted against an aggressive, well-organised and highly skilled fielding side will be aware of the pressure they put on the batsman and the effect it can have on the final result. When choosing the team, selectors should always assess the fielding capabilities of all the potential players before making a final decision. Team spirit is dependent on every member of the team, particularly the captain, being a good, if not brilliant fielder in at least one position. 'Catches win matches' is still the truest of cricket sayings.

Apart from the techniques of fielding demonstrated and described in the following photographic sequences, there are other important factors that contribute towards the make-up of the 'complete' fielder. *Physical Fitness* is essential and, just as important in the close-catching positions as it is in the outfield. Nothing looks worse than a team including players who are obviously unfit. In fact the unfit fielder is a team's biggest liability. The section on physical fitness can be studied to advantage by cricketers of all ages.

Closely allied to physical fitness is *mental alertness* and the ability to *concentrate.* However skilled one is, without concentration chances will be missed. Fielders should be thinking continually about the game, assessing the batsmen's weaknesses and anticipating the captain's moves. A study of the team's own bowlers will also add to the fielders' knowledge and effectiveness. All fielders with the exception of the close catchers should move in towards the batsman with the bowler. This enables them to move quickly towards the path of the ball as it is struck. A constant eye should be kept on the captain for field-placing changes, particularly in the middle of an over.

With all the attributes of sound technique, physical fitness, alertness and knowledge of the game, for a fielder to be recognised he must above all else practise.

Practice is the key to improvement. Remember to practise technique under pressure, physical and mental. It is easier to run out a batsman

Nothing can inspire a team more than a brilliant catch by the captain

who is halfway up the pitch when there is nothing in the game than to throw down the stumps at the bowler's end when the scores are level and number eleven batsman is a foot out of his crease, going for the winning run. It is easier to take a catch at the beginning of an innings having just gone into the field, than when one has just chased the ball to the boundary several times late in the day with the game in a tense position. In cricket as in most sports all but the soundest technique tends to collapse as concentration lapses and tiredness or stiffness set in. Be sure your practice is realistic and fun!

Finally, if you have been honoured by being selected for the team, make sure you are part of the team and not the odd man out. *Equipment* is important, its condition being more important than its cost. If a team looks the part it starts with an advantage. Don't be the one to miss a vital run-out simply because spikes are missing from your boots. Don't be the one to miss a dolly catch because you have not a cap in your bag to wear when the occasion demands. 'Sorry Skipper the sun was in my eyes', does not really cut much ice in the dressing room.

Intercepting

The technique of intercepting varies with the speed and direction of the ball and its distance from the wicket when intercepted.

A fast-moving ball in the outfield can be intercepted using the 'long barrier' method. Generally an easy 'one run', the main objective is a clean and safe stop and an early return to the wicket. This technique may be termed a defensive interception although this does not mean that from it run-outs are secondary. In fact, very often a good throw from the long barrier position can run-out the batsman trying to steal an extra run.

When it is essential for a very fast pick-up and throw, the attacking interception technique is used. Either underarm, if close to the wicket or overarm if farther away from the wicket. Accuracy is the vital aspect of throwing from these positions.

Coaching Sequence 1 (See page 58)

The 'long barrier'—Right foot and left leg form a barrier at right-angles to the path of the ball. Head over the line of the ball, fingers pointing down. From this position (with the right foot square to the target) it is natural to move into the correct sideways throwing position.

1A

Sideways position, front arm pointing to target. Eyes looking at target over left shoulder, throwing arm drawn fully back, wrist cocked and ball held in fingers.

1B

Sideways position, eyes still on target, looking over right shoulder, throwing arm fully extended to target. Left arm drawn right back past body. Full pivot on braced left leg achieved from a strong push off right foot.

Coaching sequence 1. Intercepting (long barrier)   1A   1B

Coaching sequence 2. Attacking interception   2A   2B

Coaching sequence 3. Underarm throw

3A

3B

2C

Coaching Sequence 2

Attacking interception—
Fielder moving quickly on to line of ball, balance forward.

2A

Eyes fixed on ball, right foot turning square to the line of the ball.

2B

Ball picked up in front of right foot, left leg trailing to give swing into and momentum through the throw.

2C as 1A

Coaching Sequence 3

Underarm throw—fielder moving very quickly to the ball. Balance forward and throwing arm poised.

3A

Eyes watching the ball into the hand, pick up against right foot.

3B

Early release of ball, full extension of throwing arm, eyes still on target.

Retrieving

Again when retrieving (the ball having gone past the fielder) the particular technique used depends upon the speed and direction of the ball and its distance from the wicket when retrieved.

A slow-moving or even stationary ball will be picked up against the left foot, a quicker-moving ball, against the right foot.

When the ball is retrieved close to the wicket it should be thrown 'on the turn'. When making a long throw a strong push back against the left foot will add the momentum necessary to make a strong throw without the need for a run into the throwing position (a common fault).

Coaching Sequence 4 (Slow-moving ball)

Fielder braking after fast run to the ball.

Coaching sequence 4. Retrieving (slow-moving ball)

4A

4A

Pick up against left foot, push from left foot beginning.

4B

Left leg straightening from strong push, right foot moving into square position. Throwing arm 'cocking', front arm coming round to target.

4C

Eyes now on target, sideways position achieved. Right foot beginning to push to maintain momentum throughout throw.

4D

On target, full extension of body and arms for long throw.

Coaching sequence 5. Retrieving (fast-moving ball)

4B

4C

4D

5A

5B

5C

Coaching sequence 6. Retrieving (throwing on the turn)　　6A　　6B

Coaching Sequence 5 (Fast-moving ball)

Fielder, running quickly, prepares to retrieve by moving alongside ball.

5A

Bending quickly, eyes on the ball, the left arm is already beginning to 'seek' the target area. Note that left foot has already gone through, emphasising the need for picking up against right foot.

5B

Pivot on left foot brings right leg into braking position.

5C

Momentum takes fielder on to right foot which is turning square to target. A strong push off this foot sets up a good throwing position.

Coaching Sequence 6 (Throwing on the turn)

6A

Ball picked up against right foot, left arm quickly 'seeking' target. Rapid turn and pivot on left foot commencing.

6B

Quick turn and pivot on left foot.

6C

Throwing position established.

6D

Jump off left foot enables throw of limited length to be made.

6E

Follow-through completed as weight lands on right foot— eyes still on target.

6C   6D   6E

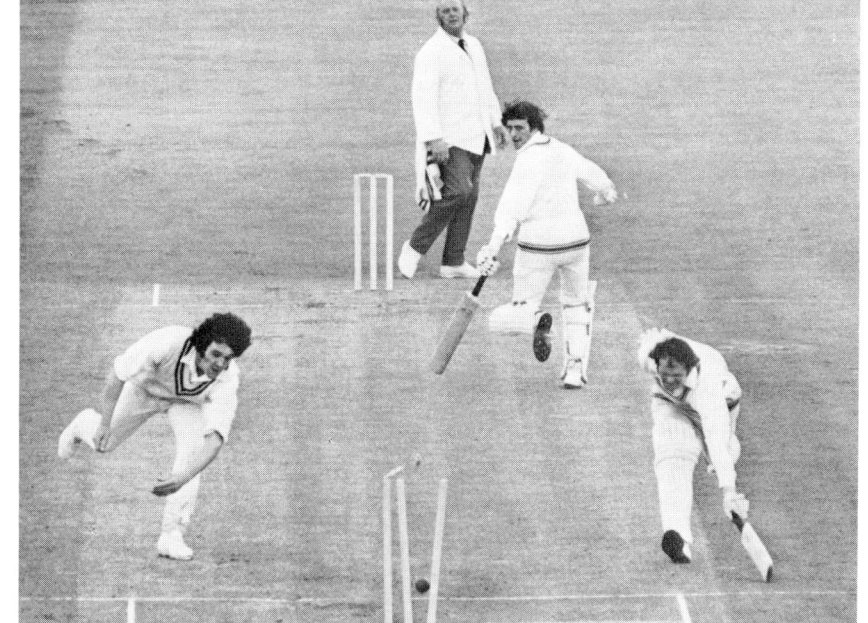

The underarm flick at the wicket by this left-handed fielder resulted in a run-out despite the batsman running his bat in correctly

Catching

'Catches win matches' is the truest of cricket sayings. Golden rules to follow are:

AWAY FROM THE WICKET

Wait until the flight of the ball has been judged and then move quickly on to the line. (Remember it is easier to run forwards than backwards.)

CLOSE TO THE WICKET

Concentrate hard on each delivery. Generally all close fielders except wicketkeeper and first slip will watch the bat. Stay down and do not anticipate.

Coaching picture 7. Close-fielding position

8 High catching

9 Flat trajectory catching

Coaching Picture 7
Eyes level, head still. Knees and hips well bent. Hands relaxed, palms facing batsman. Feet comfortably apart, weight evenly distributed.

8
High catching—Fingers spread, catch made at eye level and finally held close to chest.

9
Flat trajectory or overhead catching. Palms facing ball, fingers pointing upwards. Use hands to line up flight of ball.

A fine stumping with the minimum of movement

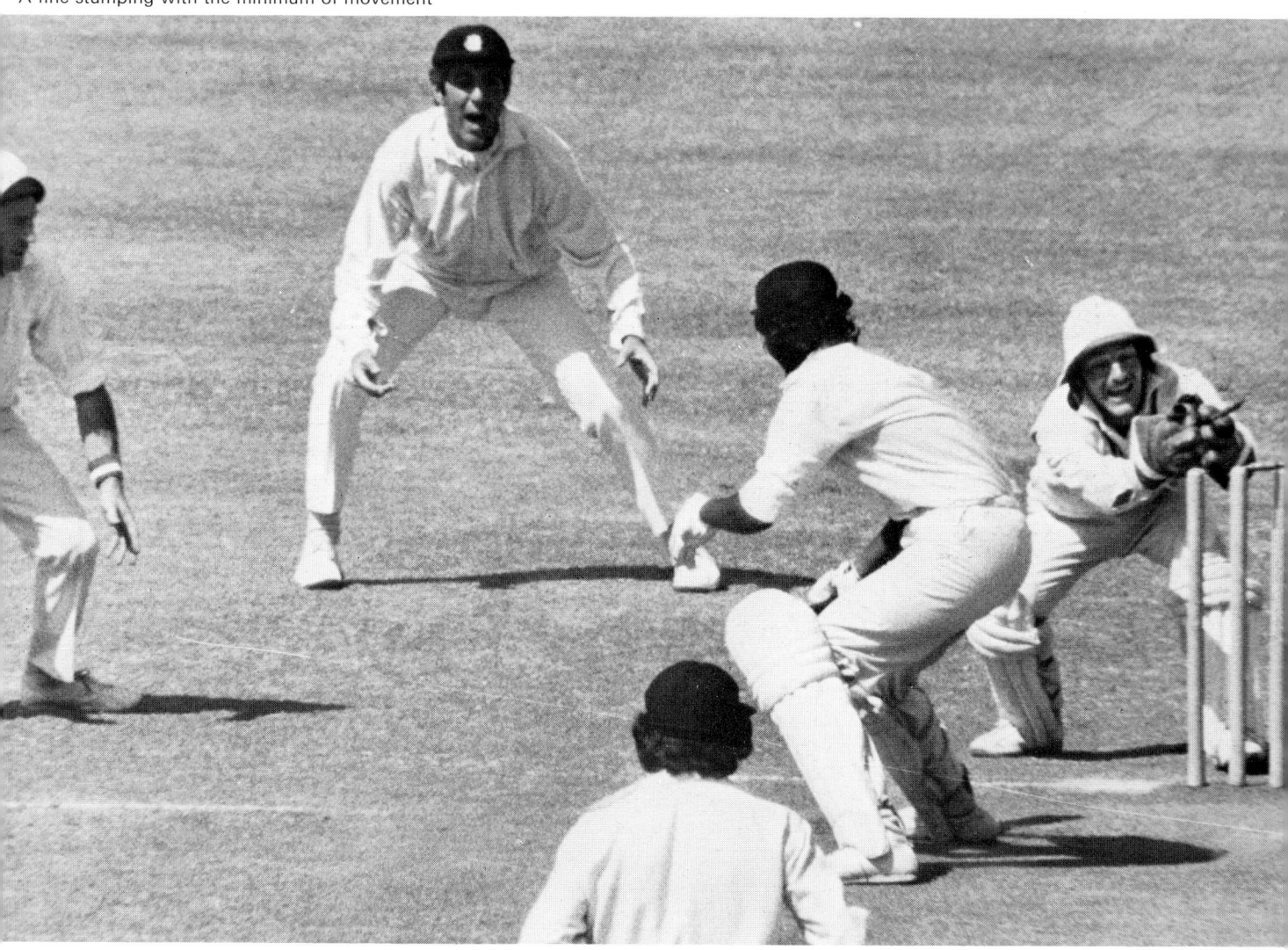

Wicketkeeping

Every wicketkeeper should remember that his first responsibility should be to assist his bowlers and thereby his team to dismiss batsmen. Towards this end the photographic sequences clearly show points of technique outside the actual taking of the ball that can make the good wicketkeeper very good and the average wicketkeeper better.

Every wicketkeeper should endeavour never to drop the ball from whatever angle it comes and regardless of where it pitches. Equally he should be aiming to maximise his chances of making a dismissal and it is this continuous maximising of chances and minimising of errors that distinguishes the top-class wicketkeeper.

Important factors in successful wicketkeeping are *good balance* and *footwork,* economy of movement and the practice of *correct techniques.*

Coaching Picture 10. Stance

Body right down with knees fully bent. Position feet to give a good view of the delivery. Head still, eyes level. Hands together, fingers pointing down, palms facing bowler. Feet comfortably apart with heels off the ground.

Coaching Sequence 11. Taking the ball standing back

Wicketkeeper forward and two full arms' length at least from first slip. Stance as when 'standing up' to the wicket in coaching picture 10.

11A

Still down but now in crouching position, poised to move to either side, with weight equally balanced on both feet.

11B

Hands coming together with palms facing ball and slightly forward to allow the hands to 'give' as the ball is 'taken', ideally between waist and knee high. Eyes still level with weight moving slightly to line of ball.

Coaching picture 10. Stance when 'standing up' to the wicket

Stumping

The sequences on pages 68–9 show the importance of good balance and footwork when looking for a very quick stumping to a ball pitched outside the off stump. Take particular note of the weight transference towards the wicket *before* the ball is taken. This makes for a very quick arm and hand action when breaking the wicket.

The ball is taken as close to the bat as possible. The wider the ball, the greater the weight transfer, moving the body off the line just before the 'take' to give greater freedom and acceleration of arm and hand movement. When taking catches, particularly off the back strokes, this movement is most useful if the ball lifts as it

12B

Moving on to the line of the ball with gloves coming together, weight is still behind the ball at this stage.

13A

Still down in the crouching position, beginning the movement towards line of ball.

Coaching sequence 11. Standing back

11A

11B

prevents the elbows from becoming 'tucked in'.

Important

Note that once the ball has been sighted the footwork is such that the eyes remain virtually on the same level until the hands are positioned for the 'take'.

Coaching Sequence 12. Taking on the off-side

Stance—without batsman.

12A

Head still down but in the crouching position, weight equally balanced until line of ball is picked up.

12C

Hands 'giving' with ball, *extremely fast weight transfer* is clearly shown with weight now coming on to left side. Head still down. The outside foot is still forward from original position and turned slightly inwards.

12D

Weight now completely on left side. Fast hand action can now be appreciated as the wicket is broken.

Coaching Sequence 13. Off-side with a batsman

Stance—with batsman.

13B

Ball keeping low, beats batsman on the drive. Hands in perfect position and having lined up with the ball, the weight is again already being transferred towards the wicket *before* the actual catching, freeing the arms for the quick movement necessary.

13C

Head right down as ball is taken.

13D

Hands move in the shortest possible time to the stumps, and a stumping looks 'on'.

Coaching sequence 12. Taking on the off-side

12A

12B

Coaching sequence 13. Off-side with a batsman

13A

13B

Remember the crease belongs to the wicketkeeper and the batsman's foot must be grounded *behind* the crease.

TAKING ON THE LEG-SIDE

Taking the ball on the leg-side when in the 'standing up' position is perhaps the most difficult technique to master in wicketkeeping. (See the sequence on pages 70–1.) A wicketkeeper is very often judged by his expertise in this aspect of the art.

12C

12D

13C

13D

Do not move from the stance position too early—before picking up the line and trajectory of the ball. Then and only then *move quickly* on to the anticipated line. Economy of movement is particularly important for consistency, as is good balance when the ball is actually taken.

Most people are either right- or left-handed, rather than ambidextrous, and it is not uncommon for experienced wicketkeepers to take the ball to the wicket with their strongest hand. This applies when taking the ball on either side of the wicket. Once used to this 'one-handed' technique of breaking the wicket it can speed up the action considerably when taking the wicket ball. It is *not* recommended that wicketkeepers 'take' the ball mainly with the inside hand as is sometimes suggested—the theory being that the thicker edge from the outside of the bat would then be covered. This method can only reduce efficiency and the total objective of endeavouring to take *every* ball cleanly. The ball should be taken naturally within the techniques noted.

Coaching sequence 14. Taking on the leg-side

14A

14B

Coaching Sequence 14. Taking on the leg-side

Line and trajectory sighted. Note: Initial movement is sideways and slightly forward.

14A

Head down, weight now on left foot as balanced weight transference takes place.

14B

Weight now on inside (i.e. right foot), eyes continuing to move on level path.

14C

Weight still on inside, assisted by right shoulder dropping. Now 'set up' for quick hand action following the 'take'.

14D

Ball about to be 'taken'. Note inward turn of left foot.

14E

Ball taken, body and hand movement towards wicket commences.

14F

Wicket broken from perfectly balanced position. Note ball in right hand.

SUMMARY

Wicketkeepers should practise taking every type of bowling and should study closely different hand and body actions. It is particularly important for the wicketkeeper to 'read' every type of delivery bowled by members of his own team. There is no reason why wicketkeepers should not take advantage of nets, where specific practice can be undertaken with or without batsmen being at the wicket. Wicketkeepers should only use nets when there is sufficient space behind the wicket and then with bowlers to whom he would normally stand up.

14C   14D   14E   14F

OTHER IMPORTANT FACTORS IN WICKETKEEPING

Run up to the wicket as quickly as possible when taking throws-in; raise an arm when at the wicket in good time. This acts as a guide for the fielder making the throw.

When returning the ball to the bowler or adjacent fielder ensure that he receives it at easily catchable height.

Once having decided (in a split second) to attempt a wide catch, do not hesitate—go all the way—one-handed if necessary!

Concentrate all the time and as the game progresses even concentrate on concentration.

COMMON FAULTS

1. Standing in 'no-man's land', neither right up nor right back.
2. Snatching or grabbing at the ball.
3. Taking one's eye off the ball.
4. Getting up too early when standing up to the wicket.
5. Moving to either side too early—before picking up the true line of the ball.
6. Excessive head movement.
7. Taking the ball off balance.
8. Incorrect weight distribution when attempting to break the wicket.
9. Casual or even lazy footwork.
10. Fingers rather than palms pointing at the ball.
11. Hesitation in going for wide balls.
12. Unnecessary use of pads.
13. Bad returns to bowler or fielder.
14. Badly cared-for equipment.
15. Loss of concentration.

Batting

Introduction

Batting is a fascinating art that is worthy of thoughtful study. Fundamental soundness of technique is essential to every batsman if consistent success is to be gained. The object of this section on batting is to analyse the principles in technique. By following the sequence photographs the co-ordinated movement will be easily understood.

When it comes to the detailed execution of the art of batting, practice at the nets is the best method of improving efficiency. So many things can be tried in the nets. You can experiment with your grip and stance, and develop, by good footwork allied to correct body and head positioning, an improvement in stroke production.

With dedicated practice a batsman should eventually

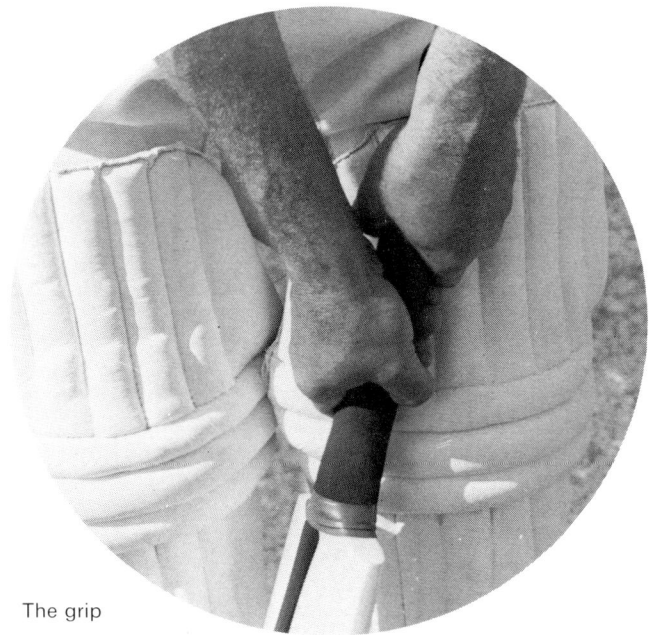

The grip

reach a stage where judgement of whether to play the ball off the front or back foot becomes instinctive rather than deliberate. The sight of a ball will trigger off a corresponding reaction so that the correct movements of head, body, feet and the bat will become almost a habit.

In the following pages the photographs are those showing strokes which are clearly and easily definable. You will also

find the mechanism of each stroke analysed step by step. Study the sequence photographs and the co-ordinated movements are easily followed.

GRIP

A correct grip is essential if the hands are to work together and so ensure contact is made with the full force of the bat irrespective of which side of the

wicket the ball has pitched. The batsman must be aware that:

- The hands are close together with the top hand near the end of the handle. The fingers and thumbs of both hands are well round the handle, with the top hand gripping firmly.
- When the bat is allowed to rest against the front pad, the back of the left hand aims somewhere between mid-off and extra-cover.
- The V formed by the thumb and first finger of the top hand is directly over the corresponding V of the bottom hand; the line of these Vs is between the the splice and outer edge of the bat.

STANCE

A correct stance is designed to allow mobility to the full. Every stroke derives most of its impetus from a sideways stance, and it conditions a correct backlift and ensures a good sight of the ball.

- Feet a comfortable distance apart, placed either side of the popping crease. The weight should be equally balanced between the feet and never on the heels: knees slightly relaxed.
- The body should be sideways.
- The head must be kept upright and turned towards the bowler, with the eyes as level as possible to command the best possible sight and judgement of the ball.
- Base of the bat should be placed just behind the toes of the back foot with the blade facing slightly towards the front leg and the hands resting on the front pad.

BACKLIFT

The principle must hold good that the straighter the backlift the better must be the prospect of the whole stroke being played straight. The bat has been picked up with both hands but with the top hand dominating. The left elbow has bent slightly and the wrist cocked, thus naturally opening the face of the bat. At the top of the backlift the left wrist is level with the left elbow, the right elbow has bent, with the right wrist a little higher than the elbow.

Forward defence

1   2   3   4   5

Forward Defence
PLAYED TO A GOOD-LENGTH BALL

1. Head and front shoulder are beginning to lead the movement of the body forward.
2. The left foot and the balance of the body are automatically following the head and front shoulder into the stroke.
3. The straight backlift has ensured that the bat, with the top hand in control, is being brought down on to the correct line of the ball. The front leg has moved out as far as possible towards the pitch and line of the ball.
4. Contact with the ball is made with the bat finishing close to the front leg which has landed slightly bent to 'shut the gate'. Top hand is completely in control, the bottom hand having been allowed to relax with a thumb and finger grip. Good contact by the hands has kept the bat at a slight angle to enable the ball to be played down.
5. Note the head position—eyes looking at the ball over the top of the bat handle as it rolls slowly away down the pitch.

COMMON FAULTS

1. Not leading with the head and shoulder.
2. Not moving the front leg far enough forward and not bending the knee.
3. Not making the left hand and arm control the stroke.
4. Not keeping the inside of the back foot on the ground.
5. Not keeping the face of the bat square to the line of the ball and the bat not travelling along it.

◀

The off-drive with a full follow-through. Note the forwards lean of the body and that the right shoulder is lower than the left

slightly over-pitched outside the off stump.

2. The front foot has landed pointing to cover. Weight has been transferred on to the front leg which is flexed at the knee. The top hand is firmly in control. The initial forward position of the left shoulder will add power and is a major factor in causing the bat to travel through the ball.

3. Contact with the ball is made close to the front foot. Note how close the right arm is to the right side as the arms and hands are being 'thrown' out in the direction the ball is to be struck. The back heel is raised but the foot has not been allowed to pivot.

4. Here the start of the follow-through shows the importance of keeping the bat continuing through the line of the intended stroke. The head has not been allowed to come up too early, since staying down in the stroke is absolutely essential.

5. The bat has accelerated down from a high backlift, through the hitting zone and here is seen continuing into the follow-through.

6. The finish of the off-drive: full follow-through; perfect poise and balance.

Drives
OFF-DRIVE

1. In the first photograph on page 77 the importance of the head leading out on to the line of the ball and the shoulder turning are clearly shown. The distance a batsman needs to advance his front foot down the pitch depends on the length of the ball, the object being to get the front foot as near to the pitch of the ball as possible. In this sequence the ball is only

The off-drive

1

2

3

4

5

6

The finish of a check-swing drive. Note that the bat is pointing down the line along which the ball has been struck. The head has been kept still

The on-drive

1   2   3   4   5

ON-DRIVE

1. As in all front-foot strokes the head and front shoulder lead the body to the line of the delivery.

2. With the on-drive there has been a slight dipping of the left shoulder and the front foot has opened up.

3. As the bat is brought down into the hitting zone the front shoulder has moved away sooner than in the straight and off drives, in order to assist the direction of the stroke. Even though the ball is being driven wide of mid-on it is important to keep the face of the bat as square to the line of stroke as possible.

4. The arms and hands are being thrown out and away from the body. Top hand has remained in control to overcome any tendency to hit across the line of the delivery.

5. Completed on-drive with a full follow-through over the front shoulder. Note that there has been no falling away of the body towards the off-side.

The straight drive

1

2

3

STRAIGHT DRIVE

1. The above sequence captures the straight drive played to an over-pitched delivery pitching close to the middle stump. The batsman is going to strike the ball between the bowler and mid-off and is seen beginning the stroke with head and front shoulder leading.

2. To ensure that the blade of the bat is kept on the path of the ball the left arm has been kept close to the body in the backlift and the right arm close to the body as the bat starts its downswing.

3. Contact is made with the ball close to the front foot. Weight is over the front leg, trunk leaning well forward and head well over the ball.

4. The arms have been 'thrown

Driving over the top

4

1

2

out' in the direction of the intended line of the stroke.

DRIVING OVER THE TOP

1. Here the batsman can be seen making a lofted drive over mid-off. The ball has been met a little earlier, at a point farther

in front of the left foot than in the case of drives along the ground. To enable the ball to be 'struck over the top', the body has been allowed to come up slightly as the bat reaches the hitting zone.

2. Both arms have followed right through the intended line of the stroke. Good arm extension into a full follow-through is of the utmost importance.

Moving down the pitch to drive

1

2

3

MOVING DOWN THE PITCH TO DRIVE

1. When the delivery is slow and its trajectory high enough to give the batsman time, he can, by moving down the pitch, turn a good-length ball into one he can drive.

2. After the initial step with the left foot, the right foot had been moved up behind it, thus keeping the body sideways to the ball and ensuring a continuing head and shoulder lead into the stroke.

3. By moving his feet correctly the batsman will reach the pitch of the ball, just outside the off stump. The basic principles of the drives will now apply. It is noticeable that the batsman has almost turned his back on the bowler with the left hip close to the intended line of the stroke.

4

5

4. The arc of the bat swing is being kept as low and flat as possible. In the timed acceleration of the bat the right hand is powerfully reinforcing the left, but on no account must it be allowed to become the dominating hand, or to shut the face of the bat before impact.

5. At the end of a well-hit drive the batsman should find himself with his weight firmly balanced on his front foot, with his head still leading, and knowing that the face of the bat has been allowed to swing down through the line in an extended and accelerated arc.

Common faults in driving:

1. Poor backlift, i.e. not picked up high enough.

2. Not leading with the head and front shoulder on to the line of the delivery.

3. In drives along the ground, not ensuring that the front foot has landed close enough to the pitch of the ball.

4. Allowing the right hand to come into the stroke too early, causing the bat to be pulled across the line of the delivery.

5. Not staying down, i.e. the head coming up before the completion of the stroke.

6. Allowing the back foot to pivot.

7. Not keeping the arc of the bat swing long, flat and smooth with the face travelling down the line as long as possible.

1

2

Back Defensive Stroke

1. From a study of these sequence photographs it will be noted that the batsman maintains a sideways position when defending his wicket against a delivery pitched just short of a length.

To enable this sideways position to be taken up a slight turning of the front shoulder can be seen as the back foot commences its movement back to land almost in line with the delivery.

2. The slight turning of the shoulder has assisted the back foot to land parallel to the crease with the head right behind the ball and still keeping its forward poise. The weight of the body is being taken up on to the back foot.

3. The full face of the bat has moved down the line of the delivery with left elbow high and with the hands slightly in advance of the blade at the moment of contact with the ball. This will enable the batsman to play the ball down. Having led, the left arm and wrist will totally control the stroke. The right hand has been allowed to relax completely into a finger and thumb grip.

4. At the finish of the back

3

4

defensive stroke it can be seen how the batsman has kept sideways, with the left foot

having followed the right, finishing in a position of natural balance close to it.

84

1

2

3

4

Forcing Shot off the Back Foot

1. A forcing shot off the back foot is the safest method of attacking a ball that has pitched short of a length on or just outside the line of the stumps, and has not bounced above stump high.

2. To play the stroke effectively the batsman, with the slight turning of the front shoulder, has taken his right foot back towards the stumps. It has landed parallel to the crease and also inside the line of the delivery, giving himself a little more 'room' than in the defensive stroke.

3. With great emphasis on the body being kept sideways, the left elbow high, the head being kept down and forward, the face of the bat has been brought down and through the intended line of the stroke. The power has come from this acceleration of the handle and the uncocking of the wrists, added to which the bottom hand has been allowed to punch through just before contact.

4. At the finish of the forcing shot off the back foot, note how the batsman has used his full height and how in its follow-through the bat points in the direction of the stroke.

COMMON FAULTS
in both the Back Defensive Stroke and the Forcing Shot off the Back Foot

1. Not stepping far enough back and across with the right foot.

2. Not landing the back foot parallel to the crease to enable the body to stay sideways on.

3. Not having a high enough backlift to enable the ball to be played down.

4. Not allowing the left hand to control the bat, thus not ensuring the bat face is kept on the line of delivery.

5. Not allowing the bottom hand to relax into a finger and thumb grip when defending.

6. Not having the front elbow high enough to enable the ball to be played down.

A magnificent example of getting behind a fast, rising ball

1

2

3

Hit to Leg
(Played to a Full Toss)

1. To ensure the perfect execution of this stroke, it must be remembered that the position of the head is of great importance. The eyes must be 'glued' to the ball and the head kept absolutely still: on no account will it be allowed to sway over to the on-side with the impetus of the stroke.

2. Having picked up the line of the delivery, the head leads the front leg, which lands with the foot pointing somewhere between cover and extra-cover, thus ensuring a firm base. The bat, from a higher backlift, is about to be brought down and across the body.

3. The ball is struck as near to full arm's stretch as possible, aiming to strike the ball in front

4

5

of square-leg, with the weight of the body being taken up on a braced front leg.

4. The bottom hand must be allowed to roll over the right,

thus ensuring the ball is struck down.

5. Throughout the stroke the head must have been kept perfectly still.

The pull

1

2

3

The Pull

1. Early judgement of the length of the delivery is vital; only the ball pitched well short of a length should be pulled. Throughout the film sequence note the stillness of the head; this will enable adjustments to be made if there are any irregularities in the bounce of the ball.

2. Using a high backlift, the batsman is taking his rear foot well back towards the stumps. The farther and earlier it moves, the longer will the batsman have to watch the ball and the greater will be his command of it.

3. To enable the body to reach a completely open-chested position, the left leg has been carried away to the on-side with the head remaining directly in line with the ball. Both feet are now almost pointing down the pitch Knees are slightly flexed to ensure the weight is kept forward.

4

5

4. A combination of wrists and arms has brought the bat down and across the body to meet the ball at full arm's stretch. In this movement the right hand has been allowed to dominate and the right wrist is just slightly shutting the face of the bat which has met the ball in a horizontal position. This, plus the transference of the weight to the left leg will ensure the ball is hit down.

5. The whole mechanism of the wrists, arms and body has been harnessed to enable the ball to be firmly struck. The more the direction of the stroke is aimed to mid-wicket the less chance there is of the batsman being late on the ball.

COMMON FAULTS

1. Not taking the back foot back and to the off of the line of the delivery.

2. Not carrying the front leg away to the on-side to open the body square to the bowler.

3. Not making sure that the head is directly in line with the delivery and that it does not turn away after the completion of the stroke.

4. Not bringing the bat down and across the body from a high backlift.

5. Not striking the ball as near to full arm's stretch as possible.

6. Hitting late and aiming the stroke too fine.

7. Not ensuring that the body weight finishes over the left foot.

The hook

1

2

3

The Hook

1. The hook shot is played to a fast short-pitched ball which has bounced at least chest high.

It is essential that the batsman moves his weight quickly on to his back foot. The backlift is made early and should be as high as possible.

2. The back foot has landed far enough across to be just to the off-side of the line of flight. The batsman by quick footwork has given himself as much time as possible to watch the ball off the pitch and has made sure that, if the ball has been missed, it would have passed over or by his left shoulder.

3. During the execution of the hook, the batsman's right foot has acted as a pivot so that, as the bat is swinging, the body has naturally moved round in a half circle with the batsman finishing up facing almost round to the wicketkeeper. He should always be looking to hook down.

The completion of the hook shot. The batsman has attempted to keep the ball down

The sweep

1

2

3

The Sweep

1. A good-length delivery bowled by a slow bowler which pitches outside the leg stump can be dealt with effectively by the execution of the sweep shot. After the initial movement of the head, the left leg, in the above photograph, is about to land in line with the delivery.

2. The front leg, having landed, is begining to bend, bringing the trunk into a slightly forward position.

3. It is important to get the bat out early on to the line of the delivery to enable it to be brought down across the body to make contact with the ball at full arm's stretch. At the point of contact the bat must be almost horizontal.

4

5

4. To make sure the ball is struck down the bat has been kept on top of the line of flight and it can be seen how the wrists have been allowed to close the face slightly.

5. Note from the photograph how still the head has been kept and how closely the ball has been watched throughout the stroke.

COMMON FAULTS

1. Not leading with head and shoulder on to the line of the ball.
2. Not landing the front foot in line with the ball and not bending knees, keeping the body too high.
3. Not making contact at full arm's stretch.
4. Not coming down on the ball.
5. Not keeping the head still at the moment of contact and immediately afterwards.

The cut

1

2

3

The Cut

1. The delivery selected to cut must be short of a length and wide of the off stump. The backlift must be high. As the line of the ball is sighted there is a pronounced turning of the left shoulder and the back foot is taken back across the wicket.

2. Most of the weight of the body has been transferred to the back foot and the turn of the shoulders has been completed.

3. From the high backlift every effort has been made to hit down at the ball which is struck almost at full arm's stretch. With the end of the blade slightly lower than the handle as the ball is struck, it is not difficult to cut downwards, thus eliminating the risk of a catch in the slips.

4

5

COMMON FAULTS

1. Not having a high backlift.

2. Not stepping across with the back foot.

3. Not turning the shoulders.

4. Not coming down on the ball with the weight on the back foot.

5. Not allowing the bottom hand to climb over the top.

4. It can be noted from the above sequence that the ball has been played behind square; in this case the ball's own momentum has been the chief source of speed off the bat.
It is vital that the body weight must be transferred to the back foot and held there as the ball is struck.

5. When cutting square, the speed of the bat action is brought about by the combination of weight transferred by the body, wrist and arms.
But in all cuts, the right hand climbs over the left and the weight goes into the stroke.

The finish of a square cut. Note the weight
fully on the back foot with the head over it

1

2

Forward Leg Glance

1. Because there is little margin
for error the forward leg glance
should not be played to a
straight ball. The most suitable
delivery for this stroke is one
that is a good length on or just
outside the line of the batsman's
pads. As with the forward
defensive stroke, the head and
front shoulder are leading the
body over and on to the line of
the delivery.
2. The front foot has landed
just inside the line of the ball so
that the ball, if missed, would
strike the outside of the front
pad. Hands are being kept in
advance of the blade to ensure
the ball is glanced downwards.
3. To enable the batsman to
have full control over the ball, it
is being met in front of the left
leg and almost directly under
the head. The wrists are being
allowed to turn the blade
slightly.
4. At the finish of the stroke
there has been no falling away
of the body towards the off-
side, and the head and trunk
have been kept in advance of
the front pad.

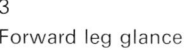
3

4

Forward leg glance

1

2

3

Backward Leg Glance

1. This stroke is played most effectively to the delivery pitched just short of a length and which is going to miss the leg stump.

In the above photograph the back foot is being taken back towards the stumps with the weight of the body being kept slightly forward.

2. The back foot has landed pointing to cover. The front foot has also been brought back to position itself just inside the line of the delivery.

The bat has been brought down close to the body with the left elbow high.

The top hand ensures the bat is kept almost perpendicular, with the handle slightly forward of the blade at contact. At this moment, the hands, with the top hand still dominant, will begin to shut the face of the bat for the required deflection.

3. From this final action photograph, it can be seen how the ball, which has been allowed to come 'right up' to the batsman, has been played down and in the direction of long leg.

COMMON FAULTS

1. Not placing the feet correctly —slightly inside the line of the ball.

2. Not allowing the ball to come up to the bat.

3. Not keeping the head and the top of the bat over the ball as contact is made.

This batsman avoids being run out by diving with his arm fully extended, and so grounding his bat behind the crease

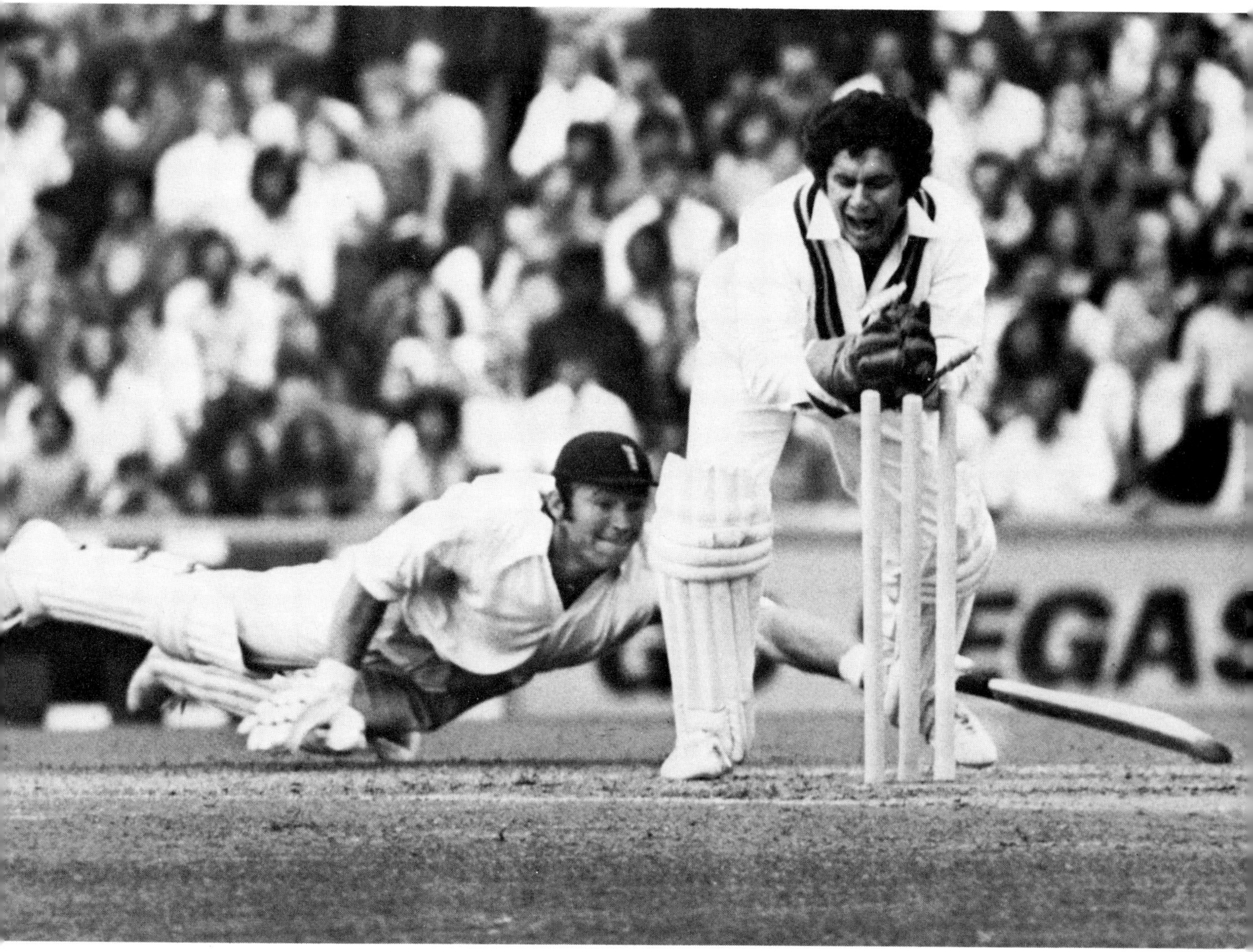

Running Between the Wickets

A cricket spectator will not experience greater excitement than when watching a partnership between two batsmen who never miss the opportunity of running quick singles. Good running between the wickets is without question a matter of judgement, experience and the batsmen having confidence in their partner's ability to respond quickly to whatever call is made.

THE CHIEF PRINCIPLES:

1. The striker is responsible for calling when the ball is struck in front of the wicket, whilst the non-striker calls for all strokes played behind the wicket. However, that must be regarded as a generalisation only. Either batsman must have the right to deny his partner's call if he considers it is too dangerous. A call, if refused, must be refused at once with a decisive NO. Once batsmen have started for a run they must go straight through with it at all costs.

2. Under all circumstances, initial calling, whether by the striker or non-striker, should be restricted to one of three calls, YES, NO or WAIT. If a call of WAIT has been made this must be immediately followed by a call of YES or NO.

3. A batsman must get into the habit of reinforcing his first call when passing his partner with a comment such as 'probably two', or 'look for three', or some such guiding remark. This situation will certainly occur when the ball has been struck through the field when one of the batsmen should be able to form a clear judgement as to whether the stroke will yield more than one run.

4. A call for a second run should be the prerogative of the batsman returning to the wicket most likely to be endangered by the fielder's throw.

5. The non-striker should always back up. This means moving a yard or so down the pitch immediately the ball has been delivered, from a position wide of the return crease on the opposite side of the stumps from the bowler.

6. When running between the wickets, a batsman must, when necessary, be prepared to change his bat from one hand to the other to enable him to watch the ball without having to look over his shoulder before turning.

7. The striker should always try to run down the side of the pitch from where the bowler has delivered the ball. But if he has moved down the pitch to play an on-drive he may then find it easier and more convenient to continue running down the on-side of the pitch. In all circumstances the non-striker's job is to give himself ample room.

8. Each batsman should ground his bat well short of the popping crease and run it in along the ground. This is particularly important when attempting to avoid a run-out or when making a quick turn for another run.

9. It is essential to run the first run as quickly as possible. This must of course be interpreted with common sense. Many strokes are played where it is highly improbable for more than a single to be scored, but even in this situation, by running and turning quickly the batsman may put the fielder under pressure, with the result possibly being a mis-field.

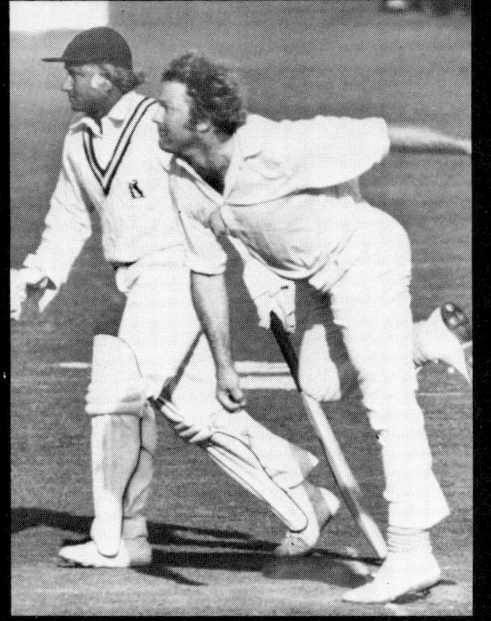

A

B

A. When backing up, have the bat grounded behind the batting crease until the bowler releases the ball

B. Move down the pitch after the ball has been delivered. Note that both the batsman and the bowler are watching the ball carefully

C. By diving, or at least stretching the arm, this batsman might have avoided being run out. Note the distance the umpire has moved from the stumps to the side on which the ball was struck, in order to be in a good position to make a decision

Some Batting Problems

When playing an innings a variety of problems are presented to a batsman. Early recognition of any problems and rapid change of method to deal with them are essential if the batsman is to succeed.

Out of touch or loss of form are terms used when a capable batsman experiences unusual difficulty in scoring runs or loses confidence to such an extent that it affects his batting technique.

When this occurs the best way to regain confidence is by playing a long innings provided the state of the game allows this. He should inspect the bowler's field carefully to discover where the chance of a quick single may be, so that the strike is given to the in-form batsman. Difficult strokes should be avoided until he feels that his confidence has returned.

Poor timing when hitting the ball may be a result of the batsman committing himself too early to a stroke off the front foot. The better players allow the ball to come very close to them so that a firm, positive and controlled stroke is played. This problem may also be caused by poor grip. The top hand must be in control, gripping the handle very firmly, so that the bottom hand cannot take charge.

Poor control of a stroke, i.e. the ball flying off the bat in the wrong direction or in the air may result from poor timing, faulty technique or bad judgement of flight. The stroke should be avoided or played sparingly until the technique can be analysed and any faults remedied in the nets. If it is merely a question of misjudging flight then try not to attack too early but again allow the ball to come up to the bat.

Hurried or rushed strokes, particularly when batting against fast bowlers, are frequently caused by late pick-up. It is good policy against all bowlers to ensure that your backlift occurs at least when the bowler is delivering the ball. If a feeling of undue haste is still felt then picking the bat up as the bowler approaches the stumps may have to be adopted.

Against real pace it is vital to ensure the bat is 'in line' with the ball. This may mean concentrating more on a lateral movement than forward or back. In addition the hands should be held high so that if the ball lifts it is still possible to play down on it.

Scoring restriction particularly by a good slow bowler with a well-set run-saving field presents a problem, even to in-form batsmen. Any player faced with this problem must be prepared to 'glide' up the pitch to attack the slower delivery. He should be prepared to sweep good-length balls which are missing the leg stump, and also to hit over-pitched balls over the top of the close field. No opportunity should be missed of taking the quick single, so that the bowler is unable to bowl to a preconceived plan at a particular batsman.

Playing a Turning Ball

A batsman cannot judge the direction or length of a delivery until the ball has been released by the bowler. When playing any type of bowler early commitment either forward or back before the ball is released can often lead to his early dismissal. A batsman may be

looking to play a certain bowler off the front foot but he must control the forward movement of his head and body until the ball is in the air.

The following are a number of points that should be put into practice when playing an off-spinner on a turning pitch.

Good length—Pitching and turning to hit the stumps.

1. The wicket must be defended by using a forward defensive stroke.

2. As contact is made with the ball, bat and front pad must be close together.

3. It is vital for the top hand to be controlling the bat, the bottom hand must not be allowed to push through.

4. Back foot may be eased along the popping crease as the stroke is played, i.e. from middle and leg guard, where both feet, in the stance position, will be outside the leg stump, the back foot, when the batsman is well forward after the completion of the stroke, will be found in line with the off stump.

Over-pitched—outside the off stump.

1. Care must be taken not to attempt to drive the ball too wide on the off side. If a batsman attempts to drive an over-pitched off-spinner through the covers there is a danger of the ball pitching and turning through the gap between bat and front pad.

2. It is far safer to drive the ball straighter, i.e. slightly with the spin.

Just short of a length

1. If the ball is pitched wide of the off stump it is prudent to avoid attempting to cut. It would be far safer to force the ball away off the back foot between mid-off and extra-cover.

2. With a delivery that pitches off stump the batsman must get right back and across his wicket seeking to defend his wicket by means of a back defensive stroke. As the ball is seen to pitch and turn, the batsman should allow his body to open up slightly, enabling him to play the ball with the spin just to the leg side of the pitch.

Long-hop The batsman must look to punish the really short-pitched delivery by playing the pull stroke, aiming to hit the ball into the area between mid-wicket and square leg.

Below are a number of further points that should be put into practice when playing a leg-spinner or a slow left-arm orthodox bowler.

Good length—pitching on the middle stump and turning to hit the off stump.

1. The batsman must play well forward and try to smother the turn.

2. If he cannot smother the turn he should not play directly at the pitch of the ball. Instead he should play forward as if the ball had pitched off stump and not on the middle stump, thus allowing the ball to turn on to the face of the bat.

Over-pitched—on or just outside the off stump.

1. These deliveries may be off- or cover-driven.

2. In driving the ball turning away from the bat every effort must be made to lean with the stroke, with the head well over the ball.

3. The left shoulder of a right-handed batsman must be turned with the head to lead with the intended line of the stroke.

4. The rear foot must not pivot.

5. The face of the bat must be kept moving down the line of the ball at the moment of contact.

The Left-Handed Batsman

The left-handed
drive

1

You will have often noticed the following phrase in coaching manuals: 'this is correct for the right-hander, but the positions should be reversed if you are left-handed'. Now, that gives the impression that the left-handed batsman and his problems are merely a mirror image of a right-hander. In fact they are faced with problems that a right-handed batsman only encounters when batting against a bowler delivering left-arm over the wicket or an off-spinner bowling round the wicket. Left-handed batsmen have always had to consider how to overcome this difficulty. They appreciate that the ball delivered by a right-handed bowler over the wicket pitching on middle and off stump around a good length or shorter, will have little chance of hitting the stumps unless it straightens after it has pitched. But while the left-handed batsman enjoys this partial immunity from being bowled or trapped lbw he is more likely to find himself edging the ball into the slip field area.

Apart from the fact that the ball is nearly always moving across the left-hander's body, he faces another serious problem seldom faced by right-handers. Despite legislation to prevent it and long examinations of the pitch by umpires followed by warnings, bowlers do tend to follow-through on the pitch after delivering the ball. In so doing they cause wear and rough. Though for the right-handed batsman this rough is harmlessly outside the leg stump, for the left-hander it can prove a major hazard. It means that the batsman must judge the line of the delivery early and know where the ball is going to pitch. This is of course important for all batsmen, but it is particularly important for a left-hander to be aware of the ball which might pitch in the rough outside his off stump and consequently do something unpredictable.

To straighten the slight angle of the ball across his body and to prevent himself making an initial early commitment on to his front foot, the top-class left-handed batsman sometimes edges across the crease, still maintaining a sideways position as he moves.

When the left-handed batsman is made to play forward, it is important that he does not attempt to play the ball too wide on the leg side, but rather develop the ability to hit the ball into the 'V' between extra-cover and wide mid-on. In this way he will be showing as full a face of the bat to the ball as possible.

2

3

4

5

6

7

Fitness and Training

To be successful in competitive cricket the player must be fit and mentally alert. Players and coaches should analyse the movement patterns in the game and base their training programme on them. Scoring single runs entails a sprint of about twenty yards which may be repeated at frequent intervals with only a small period of recovery time. Multiple runs, twos, threes, etc. require turns to be made so these also should be incorporated and different ways of completing the exercises thought up.

The simplest method is to mark out a distance of approximately twenty yards, sprint over it, slow down, turn round and then sprint back over the twenty yards to the starting place. This should be repeated several times before allowing a small rest period, after which the same number of sprints are performed again. If the players have to carry a bat and wear their pads, it is more realistic and harder work.

Competition is a great spur to most games players and the coach will find that training is tackled more wholeheartedly if it can be incorporated. Shuttle running in various types of team relay gives recovery time as well as the stimulus of competition. Fielding practice can readily be used to help improve fitness with various shuttle activities, including chasing and retrieving balls, intercepting and running to catch balls. Whenever possible a wicketkeeper should take a full part in this activity, having to run from a position some yards behind a stump to receive the return from the fielder as he reaches it.

Bowlers, particularly the quicker ones, need to be fit and strong. They should undergo the same training as other players but in addition they may also try to build up those areas of the body which they must consider to be vulnerable—groins, back, shoulders, etc. Weight training is a very useful method and they should consult someone with the appropriate knowledge in their area.

Above all, bowlers need to practise bowling off their full run, not only to become fit but to establish their rhythm in the run-up. Net bowling with only two or three bowlers per net is very demanding and a great aid to improving stamina. However, both player and coach should try to ensure that the bowler does not slip into bad habits as a result of tiredness due to over-bowling.

All players should warm up prior to a match. This may make the difference between winning or losing a match and also helps to prevent injury, particularly in hamstrings and the lumbar regions.

FOUR BASIC FITNESS EXERCISES

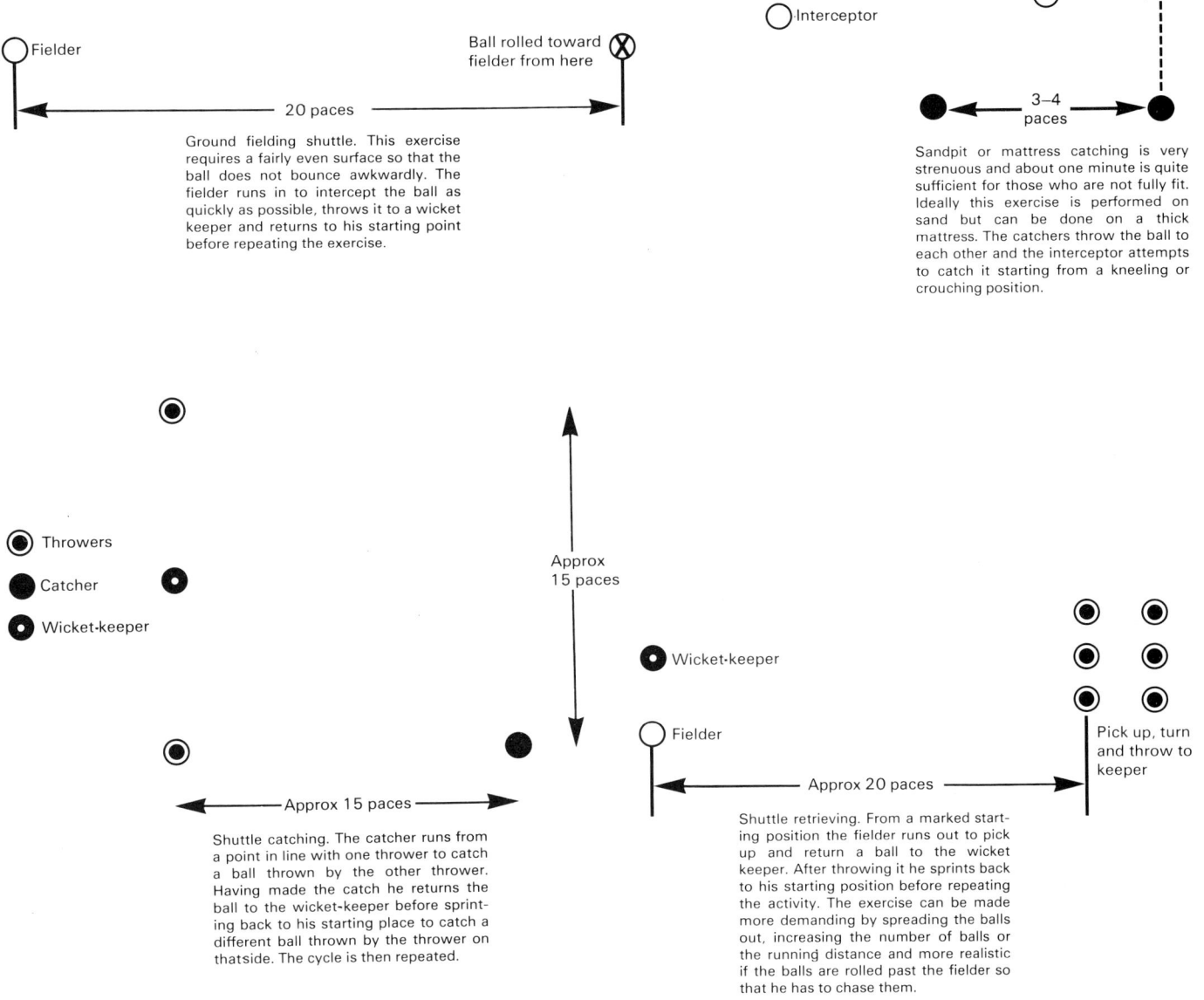

Wicket-keeper

● Starting point

○ Fielder

Ball rolled toward fielder from here ⊗

← 20 paces →

Ground fielding shuttle. This exercise requires a fairly even surface so that the ball does not bounce awkwardly. The fielder runs in to intercept the ball as quickly as possible, throws it to a wicket keeper and returns to his starting point before repeating the exercise.

● Catchers
○ Interceptor

3–4 paces

Sandpit or mattress catching is very strenuous and about one minute is quite sufficient for those who are not fully fit. Ideally this exercise is performed on sand but can be done on a thick mattress. The catchers throw the ball to each other and the interceptor attempts to catch it starting from a kneeling or crouching position.

◉ Throwers
● Catcher
◉ Wicket-keeper

Approx 15 paces

← Approx 15 paces →

Shuttle catching. The catcher runs from a point in line with one thrower to catch a ball thrown by the other thrower. Having made the catch he returns the ball to the wicket-keeper before sprinting back to his starting place to catch a different ball thrown by the thrower on thatside. The cycle is then repeated.

◉ Wicket-keeper
○ Fielder

← Approx 20 paces →

Pick up, turn and throw to keeper

Shuttle retrieving. From a marked starting position the fielder runs out to pick up and return a ball to the wicket keeper. After throwing it he sprints back to his starting position before repeating the activity. The exercise can be made more demanding by spreading the balls out, increasing the number of balls or the running distance and more realistic if the balls are rolled past the fielder so that he has to chase them.

Net Practice

The formula for a successful net session where all the batting and bowling skills can be practised will only be found if there is firstly an excellent pitch provided. The condition of a practice pitch is just as important as a pitch prepared for match play.

It is impossible for a batsman to learn a correct method and the confidence on which much of it depends, if he is asked to perform on an inadequate surface.

This will also apply to bowlers. They will only learn the subtleties of their trade on good pitches.

The nets surrounding the pitch must always be wide enough to allow a bowler, once he has delivered the ball, sufficient room to run off the pitch in his follow-through. There should also be enough room behind the stumps at the batsman's end for a wicketkeeper to practise standing up to the wicket to medium-paced and slow bowlers.

It is essential in a net practice area for the correct pitch markings to be set out as in a match. This enables the bowlers to adjust themselves to the correct interpretation of the no-ball laws. Too many bowlers get into bad habits by ignoring the crease during net practice and find to their cost that they are too frequently infringing the law when playing in matches.

Due to schools and cricket clubs having only a limited number of nets available, there is a tendency for players who are not being kept fully occupied to form groups and talk among themselves. This creates a potentially dangerous situation as they no longer concentrate on the batsman or the result of his efforts. Only a maximum number of six should be employed at one time in a net—one batting, one padding-up and four bowling. This number will allow the bowlers to get through plenty of hard work. It will also give them time between deliveries to concentrate fully before bowling another ball.

If there is a lack of discipline during a net practice a great number of bad habits could easily result. Cricketers must be made to realise that to make the best use of a net they must concentrate for all they are worth for their own benefit and for the benefit of those practising with them.

Captaincy

The ability of any individual player is closely related to his technique and whilst a study of technique forms the basis of this book, any related discourse on the playing of the game must include the application of ability within the requirements of the team, under the guidance of the captain.

The captain of a cricket team is in a position where he can influence a game more than any other player, and such is the nature of cricket, perhaps more than his counterparts in other sports. His actions both on and off the field not only significantly affect the results, but contribute directly to the enjoyment, or otherwise, of players and spectators alike. The quality of a match is more often than not dependent upon the attitudes of the opposing captains.

The captain of a cricket team is required to have many qualities, similar, but not necessarily the same, for different teams. For example, the man best suited to lead a team of highly talented, experienced players need not have the same gifts as the captain of a young inexperienced team. In general however, there are common qualities that go towards making a successful captain, providing that success is not measured only by results on the field.

Above all else a captain must earn the respect of his players. The only way to achieve this is by his unselfish performance and determined application on the field; his tolerance, understanding and good manners at all times; and by his knowledge of the game and its tactics. He will believe in discipline; when necessary to remonstrate with his players individually, he should do so in private, unless perhaps there is an example of bad sportsmanship. Whilst not necessarily the team's most skilled performer, by his good example, particularly in the field he will contribute immensely to its success.

A positive approach in endeavouring to win each match from the first ball will make every game that much more interesting and enjoyable. At the same time it is the captain's prerogative to play the game as he sees it and if he feels after striving for a win that it is not possible, his next objective will be not to lose. The captain of a team must never forget that he occupies a most privileged position to which he has been elected as being the best man for the job. As such, whilst it is his duty to captain the team to the best of his ability, he should also remember that he is responsible for transmitting the policy of those that elect him on to the field of play. Whatever the actions of his team and himself, both on and off the field, they serve only to credit the club, school or other organisation they represent.

It is hoped that these notes have clearly stated what is generally expected of the team's captain. Most of the qualities noted are, in fact, inborn. For example, welcoming the opposition, thanking those, very often behind the scenes, who

Every player should earn the respect of his team-mates. Here Bob Taylor shows agility, expertise, fitness and enthusiasm as he stumps M. J. Smith after taking a wide leg ball

have contributed to the match are natural gestures of the good captain and simply come under the heading of good manners. In the actual playing of a match, however, experience and a knowledge of good tactics are a necessary complement to other attributes and are assets that can be acquired. It is appropriate therefore that in analysing the techniques of playing we should also look in depth at what, in the light of experience, are good tactics.

Prior to the Match

A good captain will be well-read in the game and have a good knowledge of the laws. Experience is an asset but everyone must begin somewhere and if limited in experience he will be helped by having a good appreciation of technique in all skills. Simply by the reading and study of publications such as *The M.C.C. Coaching Book* and *The Laws of Cricket* he will acquire a confidence born of sound knowledge.

The young captain in particular should avail himself of all advice he can get and assess its value in retrospect. One need never stop learning about the game of cricket.

Through practice and discussion with his team the captain should be well armed with practical knowledge well before the game. He will be well aware of the abilities of every one of his players and will have instructed them, perhaps in co-operation with an experienced coach or adviser, in many aspects of the game in which team-work is essential. For example, everyone should know all the fielding positions for different bowlers and the importance of watching the captain for field-changing signals. The team will be expected to look like a team when they take the field and not as is sometimes seen—a collection of odd cricketers dressed in different caps and sweaters, leaving the pavilion in ones and twos!

In practice sessions the captain will use his influence in a number of ways. He will, in co-operation with the groundsman, have ensured the practice pitches are as good as possible and that those using them do so in an intelligent manner. Hard fielding practice will be a 'must' in any practice session. He will ensure that all members of the squad will get equal opportunity of good practice and vary the order of practice accordingly. Specific fitness training should be considered separately to skills practice, and training programmes to suit individual players can be devised in co-operation with specialists. There can be great fun in training sessions and fully fit cricketers are better cricketers!

The captain should automatically be a member of any 'Selection Committee' but should remember that it is not his prerogative to select the team himself. Others will very often have greater knowledge of 'fringe' or new players. At the same time he should have great influence on selection as he will have witnessed individual performances at close quarters —under pressure, which is the true test of a cricketer's ability. It is the captain's responsibility and a very important one, to speak with the players not selected for the team. He must be honest but kind in his approach and must have words of encouragement and advice. If a player has been dropped from the team for reasons other than playing performance the captain will need to be equally honest and explain exactly to the offender why he is not in the team.

Prior to a match, discussion of tactics can never go amiss, providing the captain feels that it can serve a useful purpose.

Bearing in mind the possible playing conditions and knowledge of the opposition, the captain can inform the team of his general plan of campaign. They will in turn be required to add to the meeting in the light of their own experience and ideas. Once the match has commenced there must be no doubt as to who is the leader and every player should understand that as a member of the team he must back the leader 'to the hilt'.

To Bat or to Field?

This decision depends on the type of game, the comparative strength of the teams, the state of the pitch and the type of weather likely to occur during the match.

As a general rule when winning the toss on a firm pitch with a reasonably experienced side and no rain expected, a captain will elect to bat first. The pitch is generally at its best early in the match and the ball's behaviour after pitching may be predicted with reasonable accuracy. In afternoon or one day matches little wear or change will be noticed if the pitch has been prepared well.

Should a pitch be damp, soft or loose on top, the surface may not withstand the impact of the ball and pieces may be taken out by the ball, causing it to bounce unpredictably. Under these conditions batting is difficult, but may become even more so if the pitch is drying out under a hot sun. Once again a captain should have little hesitation about batting first.

Knowledge of individual grounds and the characteristics of their soils is a great help in making the decision. Some pitches, especially those on sandy soils, dry out quickly and may cause batsmen serious problems for only a short time.

When the pitch is sodden and there is a great deal of surface moisture on the outfield, the ball quickly becomes wet. It is then difficult for bowlers, whether fast, medium or spin, to grip the ball firmly. Many bowlers cannot bowl with their usual accuracy nor can they make the ball swing or spin appreciably when it is so affected. Although the ball will not run quickly over the outfield, the batsmen still have the advantage over the bowlers because of the ease in predicting the path of the ball.

To invite the opposition to bat first may indicate that the team considers itself strong in batting but weak in bowling and therefore believes that the best possibility of winning is to 'chase runs'.

Another reason may be that although the pitch is hard, the grass has not been cut short making it a pitch which will allow the ball to 'seam' off it— move to the off or leg because the seam of the ball has obtained a purchase from contact with the grass. A captain can discover this possibility by rubbing his thumb along the surface of the ground and simulating the ball pitching. A green stain from the grass on the thumb can be a reasonable indicator. So, providing he has good seam bowlers, he may decide to field first. Conversely, if he is lacking bowlers of this type and the opposition have good ones, the decision to field may still be made as a pre-emptive move, denying the use of the new ball to the opposition when the pitch is likely to be most responsive. As the day wears on, the grass will begin to lose its moisture and later the pitch will be more docile, particularly if only one new ball is used for the entire match, instead of one per innings.

Showery weather presents a captain with a very difficult decision. A heavy shower on a firm pitch may make the ball lift viciously if it only softens the top. A prolonged shower may wet the pitch below the top layer and so deaden the pitch, making the batting easier. Local knowledge gained only through experience, and the ability to forecast rainfall together with its effect on a particular pitch, are almost a necessity for a captain to make the correct decision consistently. A useful maxim is when in doubt bat!

The Fielding Captain

It is in the field that the captain can perhaps make his greatest contribution towards the winning of a match.

As the team takes the field the captain will have in his mind a general tactical plan. At the same time he will be conscious that it may be necessary to change tactics at any time. He must realise that if the ground is hard and fast his fielders can be deployed that much deeper and finer (i.e. not so square to the wicket) to take catches and save runs. Conversely if the ground is slow, fielders will be closer and squarer to the wicket. 'Halfway positions' where fielders are too deep to save a single or too close to cut off fours should be avoided. Each opposing batsman should be studied separately and the field set accordingly. At the same time, the captain should not be constantly changing his field significantly, except in the case when a left-hander is at the wicket. Even then, if all the fielders are well drilled and on their toes, this need not be a time-consuming change-over. Neither need the tactics of opening up the field to an attacking batsman and closing up for a defensive batsman. Whenever possible specialist fielders, i.e. slips, short-legs, cover-point, should be placed in their special positions, but never should they be allowed to feel that they can not be required to field in any position. Specialist bowlers should be protected to some degree from too much running and throwing as this can only reduce their effectiveness in bowling. If the captain is himself a specialist fielder, unless his concentration for captaincy is affected, he should retain his position.

Nothing can inspire a team more than a brilliant catch by the captain! Whilst the captain need not field in any particular position he should avoid the outfield as he would find it difficult to 'manage' the game and communicate with the bowlers.

The captain must always ensure that the game 'flows' whether attacking or defending. Time wasting in any form is to be deplored as it detracts from the game and it should be remembered by all that wickets can only be taken and runs scored when the ball is in play.

In deciding the tactics to be employed against any particular batsman the fielding captain should be very observant. He will look for signs of nervousness or over-confidence in the batsman, and in particular for faults in technique. In every case he will communicate with his bowlers in an effort to take full advantage of any weakness.

The wicketkeeper can be a very useful ally, as from his position he can observe many useful points that others in the field may not be aware of. A good guide to where in the field the batsman will tend to hit the ball can be obtained by noticing the batsman's grip.

The batsman whose grip is towards the bottom of the handle will usually tend to play the cut and the pull shot. That is, the ball will be hit generally off his back foot, square and behind the wicket. Players who hold the bat with hands together towards the top of the handle will tend to be drivers of the ball and hence the captain can look for the ball being hit straighter. The batsman whose top hand grip is such that the back of the hand is behind the handle when playing at the ball will generally be defensive. Hence he can be attacked with full-length bowling. Such knowledge and more importantly experience of particular batsmen can only

assist the captain in applying tactics and using the bowlers likely to be most effective.

The state of the pitch is perhaps the most significant factor in final team selection, bowling and fielding tactics. Only experience can tell the captain exactly how best to cope with the particular conditions, but a good knowledge of his bowler's capabilities and temperaments will be a tremendous advantage.

Overbowling key bowlers, particularly early in the game, is a common fault of inexperience on good pitches. On bad pitches, it is important to recognise the point at which a key bowler has lost his penetration and is in danger of letting the batting side off the hook. On this type of pitch it is generally good tactics to let his key bowlers at least get to this point, as there is an equal danger that too early a change will give the batsmen respite and extra confidence. On a bad pitch it is likely it will be only necessary to use three or even two bowlers to dismiss the batting side. Another fault of inexperience on all pitches is the habit of using all one's bowlers before returning to the key bowlers.

The captain should expect accuracy in length and direction from his bowlers and never be persuaded to set a field for the bad ball. If there are too many of these a change of bowler is the only answer. When conditions are in favour of the batting side the captain should remember that variety can help. He should try to avoid using the same type of bowler from both ends. A good ploy can be to bring back the key bowler just prior to an interval so that after the interval he can continue. The intervening rest enables him to bowl a longer and more effective spell.

The Batting Captain

Whereas in the field the captain's job is very practical, when batting he reverts to the role of adviser, psychologist and mathematician! When batting himself, he must be certain to try and play the type of innings required by the situation and so set an example to the team.

A settled batting order is desirable with every batsman made aware of the responsibilities of his position. It is the job of the opening batsman to establish a platform from which the bowling can be attacked and a good score achieved in the shortest possible time. There is no reason why opening batsmen should not be stroke-makers but it should be remembered that they have the task of facing the best fast bowlers at their freshest with a new ball. Nos. 3 and 4 are generally the team's best batsmen and quickest scorers. Nos. 5 and 6 will be versatile in approach, being adaptable to the needs of the situation they are confronted with. The batting order from Nos. 7 onwards is usually made up of bowlers and the wicketkeeper but this does not mean they should consider themselves incapable batsmen. In fact the success of a team can depend on the runs contributed by the so-called non-batsmen, all of whom should be encouraged to improve with practice and opportunity.

It is always useful if one or two left-handed batsmen are in the team, particularly when batting with a right-hander. The change for the bowler can be disturbing and may open up scoring opportunities if his length and line vary because of the different angle he is required to bowl.

The captain should always sit with his team during the innings. As the game progresses he can then encourage the ingoing batsmen should he feel it necessary, just as he can commiserate with the incoming batsman should he have been dismissed for a low score. The captain should take every opportunity of praising a good innings, even though it may may have been a short one sacrificed for the needs of the team. The captain should never remonstrate with a batsman who is out to a poor stroke. Mistakes can be analysed later should it be necessary. If a batsman has deliberately ignored instructions against the interests of the team, this is a different matter and he should be made aware of the consequences of his folly, in private preferably. In general it is best to allow batsmen to play their natural game for which they were selected.

When chasing or building up a total, however, this is not always possible and it sometimes falls to the lot of the middle order or later batsmen to sacrifice their wickets in pursuit of quick runs. This particularly applies when the policy (a very good one) of obtaining a sound start to an innings is followed. With wickets in hand, the advantage can easily swing to the batting side in a tight game, as bowlers become tired or discouraged by lack of immediate success.

Experience will give the captain the knowledge of when to make a declaration as this can depend on so many factors, i.e. time available, the state of the pitch, the quality of the opposition, etc. The timing of a declaration is one of the most important decisions of a captain as it can influence the game and the result so much. The captain should be looking to ensure that the opposing team feel that they have a chance of winning. If he declares without leaving some sort of chance, particularly on a good pitch, the game stagnates and the chances of a victory are greatly reduced. If, having made a reasonable declaration and because of the fall of an early wicket or two, the batting side look like 'closing up' and playing for a draw it can be sound captaincy to open up the game again by ensuring that the batting side 'catch up' to some degree. When batsmen are looking for runs so the chances of claiming their wickets increase.

One feature of a successful and entertaining team that seems to stand out when they are batting is the running between wickets. This can be a major factor in their success and the captain should encourage his team to be constantly looking for quick runs. Not only does it keep the scoreboard ticking over but it can have a demoralising effect on the fielding side. Confidence in each other stemming from overall team spirit is the secret of good running between wickets.

Conclusion

Very often someone with all the qualities of a good captain is not elected simply because he is a specialist bowler, a wicketkeeper or an outstanding close-to-the-wicket fielder. The reason is that it is thought that the concentration required for captaincy in the field is best left to a batsman who is not required to divide his concentration to the same extent as those who specialise in the field. There may be some truth in this but it should not be the criterion in selecting the man for the job.

The Spirit of Cricket

As this publication is unquestionably a treatise on the techniques of playing the game of cricket one might wonder as to why it is necessary to conclude with a chapter entitled 'The Spirit of Cricket'. The answer is that cricket, whilst being a game, is also much more. To many it is a way

of life and for those who play and watch, not only does the excellent performance of its skills give pleasure, but equally so does the involvement in its folklore. Cricket has been with us for over four hundred years, yes, four hundred years, and to ignore this incredible fact in discussing the techniques of the

game as it is now would only be a dis-service to those whom we wish to encourage. Cricketers will tell you that whatever its limitations, and over the centuries there have been many, cricket has one outstanding feature—and that is, it produces characters, many of whom in the passage of time have left indelible memories that can be treasured and enjoyed wherever the game is played. Such names as W.G. Grace, Spofforth, Barnes, Jessop, Hobbs, Hendren, Trumper, Hammond, Larwood, Bradman, Tate, Headley and more recently Compton, Hutton, Evans, Bedser, Harvey, Trueman, Worrell, Weekes, Statham, Benaud, Sobers, May and Cowdrey to name but a few of the more famous, are still with us. How lucky these men are and yet how fortunate are we to be part of the heritage that they and others like them created. Whatever the future holds for every cricketer that reads, practises and benefits from the lessons contained in this book let them be assured of one thing—they will be discussed and compared with their counterparts of the past, regardless of their techniques or the level at which they play and in this way will themselves contribute to the enchantment of this game of cricket.

Having stressed the importance of the past and what can be its effect on the future, cricket today has much to cope with. Many other sports and pastimes have emerged to compete with cricket for the time of youngsters and adults alike. The economic problems of providing facilities and encouragement are considerable but the game still has much

to offer. Those in cricket with the interests of youth and the game at heart have, whilst retaining its inherent spirit, developed it in such a way that it can provide all the requisites of the modern healthy youngster. Whilst cricket in the past has always been a game contested between two teams of eleven players, today when time and space are limited, variations on the original game have been instituted. 'Six-a-side' and other forms of cricket are now very much a part of junior competition and along with such developments, coaching of youngsters is now organised to provide a more stimulating exercise for all those involved.

For those who watch the game at adult level, administrators have developed matches that are played over differing periods of time; from one-day forty overs per side matches to five-day Test Matches. Each type of game has its following amply demonstrated by the large numbers that attend, watch on the TV screen or listen to the radio.

With this encouraging background today's players— and perhaps more important, tomorrow's players—have a most serious duty in ensuring that they play the game in a manner which not only befits its traditions, but measures up to its challenge of the future.

Cricketers should pay heed to the fact that the game is after all a recreation and that good manners, patience, tolerance and chivalry are the true attributes of its players. A good team must strive for victory from the very first ball, with intelligent application, concentration and team spirit.

Attack, whether batting or fielding, should always be the foremost consideration, and if at the end of a match both teams can feel they have been playing together, rather than against each other, the game will have benefited.

One of cricket's most appealing features is that it offers recreation and the opportunity of success to different types of individuals. Whereas in many sports physical conformity in terms of strength or shape can be a pre-requisite for participation, and certainly success, cricket caters for the widest possible variation in physical characteristics. Tall, short, fat, thin, strong or not so strong; all have a place in the team, if by practice and enthusiasm they learn the game's lessons.

Whilst this book is produced primarily as an aid to understanding the game's techniques, the application of these techniques can only be successful if they are applied within the spirit of the game.